It's God's War

A Biblical View of SPIRITUAL WARFARE

by

Judson Cornwall

 It was originally published in England by Sharon Publications under the title *Whose War Is It, Anyway?* This revised edition has been totally retypeset.

McDougal Publishing is a ministry of The McDougal Foundation, Inc., a Maryland nonprofit corporation dedicated to spreading the Gospel of the Lord Jesus Christ to as many people as possible in the shortest time possible.

Published by:

McDougal Publishing
P.O. Box 3595
Hagerstown, MD 21742-3595

visit our website: www.mcdougal.org

ISBN 1-884369-86-3
(Previously 1-871376-166)

Printed in the United States of America
For Worldwide Distribution

Dedication

To pastor Glenn Foster and his wife, my daughter Dorothy, and their precious church family at Sweetwater Church of the Valley in Glendale, Arizona.

Be not afraid nor dismayed by reason of this great multitude; for the battle is not yours, but God's.

2 Chronicles 20:15

CONTENTS

PREFACE

As young David stood facing Israel's national enemy, the Philistine giant, Goliath, he was aware of the great fear which held the armies of Israel in its grip. The consequences of losing the fight with this giant would be far-reaching, yet David was not afraid and declared, *"The battle is the LORD's."* He refused to be overwhelmed with the odds, for he had learned that God is always victorious, and that those who love and serve Him are always victorious as well.

I have been troubled in recent years to see the emphasis being placed on Satan and his demons, as if they were so great that we should suddenly fear them. I cannot accept it, for Christ has promised us *"power over all the power of the enemy"* and that *"nothing shall by any means hurt [us]"* (Luke 10:19).

During the early days of the Pentecostal movement in this century, casting out demons was a common practice when praying for the sick. It was an accepted part of dealing with sickness. The emphasis, however, was not on the power of demons, but on the power and presence of Jesus.

Over the years, the emphasis on casting out demons declined until we experienced a wave of divine healing campaigns following the Second World War. During this movement, emphasis on the demonic was revived.

Although healing through faith in God's provision was the prime emphasis, demonic activities and our power over them was highlighted.

A decade or so later, after the healing campaigns declined, we had what I consider to be an overemphasis on resisting the devil in what some evangelists called "deliverance services." These ministers saw demons as the root cause of every problem. This proved to be a popular theme, for people flocked to those crusades from many places, just to be "delivered" from demon influence. Healing was usually a by-product of this ministry. Deliverance from demons was the main product.

Some twenty years later, in the early days of what has come to be known as the Charismatic movement, a more extreme version of this overemphasis on the demonic came into vogue in some circles. Some special crusades had believers spitting their demons into paper bags, and books on the subject of everything from pimple demons and ugly demons to body odor demons were widely praised as having the answer for our every problem. Many believers began to see demons behind every tree and rock, to give the demons names and to speak often about them to others.

After this had gone on for a while, however, people seemed to come to their senses and to realize that in Christ none of these supposedly terrifying forces has any power over us. We need not concentrate on demons or their activities, nor spend our time worrying about how to overcome them, for Christ has overcome them, and through Him we are *"more than conquerors"* (Romans 8:37).

In recent years, however, we have entered into another round of overemphasis on the power of Satan and demons. This time the teachings carry the label of "spiritual warfare." The emphasis is not primarily for the sick and suffering, nor for individuals bound with evil spirits, but concerns itself with taking authority over "ruling spirits" over cities and nations. This is a popular theme that draws crowds and gets newspaper space and television coverage.

I am fully aware of Paul's challenge to the Church:

> *Put on the whole armour of God, that ye may be able to stand against the wiles of the devil. For we wrestle not against flesh and blood, but against principalities, against powers, against the rulers of the darkness of this world, against spiritual wickedness in high places.* Ephesians 6:11-12

The full armor that Paul was describing here, however, was defensive, not offensive armor. The offensive action we are to take follows:

> *Praying always with all prayer and supplication in the Spirit, and watching thereunto with all perseverance and supplication for all saints;*
> Verse 18

The offensive action required of every believer includes praying, supplicating, watching and persevering. In my view, however, we must direct all these actions to God, not to Satan. As Christians, we relate to Christ Who has won a complete victory over Satan. He did not commission us to defeat the devil on His behalf. Yet some have taken Paul's teachings and used them for an extreme emphasis that is neither healthy nor helpful. The passage that has been misused more than any other is this:

> *(For the weapons of our warfare are not carnal, but mighty through God to the pulling down of strong holds,) Casting down imaginations, and every high thing that exalteth itself against the knowledge of God, and bringing into captivity every thought to the obedience of Christ.* 2 Corinthians 10:4-5

It seems clear to me that Paul was speaking of taking control of our thought patterns, where Satan directs his greatest attacks. If we can bring our thoughts into obedience to the Word of God, we can defeat the devil, pull down his every stronghold in our own minds, and live in the victory Christ died to provide for us. No other warfare is necessary.

For a long while, I resisted every urging to write a book on this subject, for I was sure that this fad, like others before it, would eventually exhaust itself. Those who had heard me preach on Christ's victory, however, pressed me almost mercilessly to write what God was showing me. When the book was first published in England and I brought copies to this country, they were exhausted very quickly. The book was well received by some and greatly resented by others.

As this revised edition comes to press, I can only urge you, the reader, to keep an open mind as you explore its pages. I believe that my years of experience can help to save many young Christians from some very serious pitfalls.

Let me say at the outset that I believe in deliverance from demonic power; I carry an authority over the satanic and have exercised it repeatedly. The difference in my approach to deliverance and that which is popularly preached today is that I operate on the basis of the finished work of Christ at Calvary. I always deal with God, not with Satan, for I feel no need to destroy Satan's kingdom before God's can be built.

I believe in praise and worship, I practice it privately and publicly, and have written several books on the subject. I do not, however, see worship primarily as a means of battling my enemies. My worship, in whatever form it may be expressed, is directed exclusively to God. If, while I am worshiping the Lord, demon spirits feel that they must flee the heavenly atmosphere created by my praise, so be it. That is often the by-product of praise, but I will never allow it to become the main focus. I am not here only to do battle with demons; I am here to worship God. After all, *It's God's War*.

Judson Cornwall
Phoenix, Arizona

Chapter 1

Whose War Is It, Anyway?

But thanks be to God, which giveth us the victory through our Lord Jesus Christ.

1 Corinthians 15:57

In far too many Christian circles today, the emphasis being placed on the devil and demons is extreme. More can be heard, in some meetings, about Satan, demons, and dark principalities than about the Lord Jesus Christ Himself. Far too much emphasis is being placed upon the power vested in us as individual believers rather than the power of the blood of Jesus Christ to overcome every evil. There is absolutely no biblical basis for many of the activities upon which modern believers are concentrating their time and energy.

We have the finished work of the cross, so why should we insist on doing something to help God bring redemption to our souls? God's grace is still sufficient for every sin. Just as we need not do anything to punish ourselves for wrongdoing, we also need not do anything to liberate ourselves from it. God is still God, and we must stop trying to do His work for Him.

In one sense, what is happening today is nothing new. Many years ago, when I was still pastoring, our young people returned from a youth camp filled with enthusiasm and zeal. We made room for their testimonies during the Sunday night service, and one young lady said, "Pastor, we've received something powerful from God. Relax. We'll bring this church to real victory for you." I knew in that moment how God must feel when we try to do everything in our own strength. We're like the flea on the head of the elephant. Just after the elephant had crossed an aging bridge, the flea, who had enjoyed the ride immensely, whispered into the elephant's ear, "Wow! Didn't we shake that bridge!"

We are benefactors of Christ's sacrifice

If we were capable of self-liberation, God would have sent an angel to instruct us in self-deliverance. He could have told us how to do it through one of the many mighty prophets He used to speak to Israel. He didn't do that. Instead, Almighty God sent us His Son to become the Redeemer of all mankind. Even a casual reading of history proves that man is capable of self-destruction, but incapable of self-deliverance.

The prophet Isaiah saw the fruitlessness of the efforts of men and women to produce victory. In the imagery of childbirth he wrote:

> *We have been with child, we have been in pain, we have as it were brought forth wind, we have not wrought any deliverance in the earth; neither have the inhabitants of the world fallen.* Isaiah 26:18

Our relationship with God has implanted a divine life within us, but instead of delivering a child of worship, praise, and adoration, we choose to spend our time pursuing enemies—real and imagined.

Should we care that people spend their time in such pursuits? After all what harm is done? The truth is that there are sad results and many casualties resulting from these "wars." When young believers have their hopes dashed again and again, some suffer emotional damage. Some, through their repeated failures to achieve what has been promised them, actually have their faith undermined. What's worse, some, because of their misdirection, have not learned to face the true enemy, and he has conquered far too many of them.

During the Iran-Iraq War, it horrified us to see thousands of young Iraqi boys being sent into battle ahead of the trained soldiers as though they were a legitimate part of the army. They had been promised eternal pleasure if they were killed, but no one told them that their true purpose was to sweep a particular area of land mines and to draw enemy fire so that the real troops could more readily gain the upper hand. Unseen mines blew apart hundreds of those deluded boys, but Iraqi army officials continued to send more. Someone had decided that young men were cheaper and more expendable than mine sweepers. I see a parallel in what is happening in the spiritual realm. Young believers, having been told that they can unseat authoritative spiritual forces in the heavens, are being blown away by hidden land mines.

Some of the childish activities of modern saints have provided the media an opportunity to make Christians look like fools. Where is the proof? reporters want to know. While the claims of victory have been great, there is no evidence to back up those claims. If spiritual forces are being bound, cast down or destroyed, should there not be some visible evidence of it in the community? Should not someone outside of the close-knit fellowship of our Christian magazines be reporting this phenomenon?

I am old enough to remember the great Smith Wigglesworth, Aimee Semple McPherson and Dr. Charles Price. In many places, their Christ-centered ministry closed bars, theaters, and other places of worldly amusement. Policemen often attended the special revival services these men and women conducted, for there was no criminal activity to guard against because of the spiritual awakening their ministry brought to a community. Where righteousness reigns, unrighteousness is reined in. True warfare occurs when we exalt Christ in righteousness and faith. Isaiah put it this way:

> *With righteousness shall he judge the poor, and reprove with equity for the meek of the earth: and he shall smite the earth with the rod of his mouth, and with the breath of his lips shall he slay the wicked.*
> Isaiah 11:4

This prophet, who had seen the Lord in His holy Temple, also said:

> *The work of righteousness shall be peace; and the effect of righteousness quietness and assurance forever.* Isaiah 32:17

It has been repeatedly testified that communities

where Dr. Charles Price held extensive campaigns had a window of Heaven open over them for many years afterward. I enjoyed attending many of his conferences and can testify to the amazing power of God that flowed through him in healing waves and in delivering power. For a time I pastored in a community where he, years before, had conducted a lengthy campaign. I can testify that what people were saying about his long-term impact upon a community was true.

A similar testimony can be given of Sister McPherson. As despised as she was by the press, the members of the media had to admit that wherever she went, she disturbed the status quo. When these ministers of God went into an area with the Gospel, it produced visible effects that even the non-Christian press was forced to report.

If modern testimony is not enough, we can look to Bible history found in the Sacred Scriptures. The Apostle Paul disturbed every community he visited, even if he was there for just a short time. He was a blessed troublemaker. His success was not, as some have indicated, because he wrestled constantly with demons wherever he went. Paul proclaimed a positive Gospel, not a negative one. He did not teach that we must defeat every enemy, but that Christ has already won that victory for us. He said: *"But thanks be to God, which giveth us the victory through our Lord Jesus Christ"* (1 Corinthians 15:57). The work we do for the Gospel should produce lasting results. Crime should be dramatically lowered in our communities and church attendance dramatically raised.

When the United States was pulled into the war in

Vietnam, many considered that it was not our war and that our doing poorly there was a direct result of that fact. Could it be that our spiritual leaders are drawing us into another Vietnam? If the age-old conflict is between God and the devil, why do we insist on getting caught in the middle of it?

I have never been comfortable with the teaching that God needs us in His army. The conflict Satan initiated in Heaven will not be resolved by either he or God recruiting more soldiers to stand on their respective sides. God did not create us just so that we could help Him outvote those who choose the satanic kingdom, and He did not create us to out-fight them either. He created us to dwell in a living and loving relationship with Him and to praise and worship Him. When we misdirect the loving energy of God's redemption, we frustrate the very purposes for our creation and recreation. God did not make us for fighting; He made us special creatures of His love.

We are creatures of God's love

Love and warfare do not harmonize. The passion of war is hatred. One of the first tasks in military boot camps is to infuse the new recruits with hatred for their enemy. When rightly stirred, hatred can be a strong motivating force. When misdirected, it can be a destructive power—especially in the one who is filled with the hatred.

Often when leaders bring congregations into warfare, the people release deep feelings of anger, frustration, and hatred. Instead of these feelings going to the cross for cleansing, they are repeatedly expressed over and over again.

Some leaders constantly dwell on the evil of Satan's character, encouraging their members to vent their feelings of anger toward him through vocal badgering or heckling. Some are encouraged to stomp the devil under their feet. These activities do release anger, but anger needs to be requited not released, and only the work of Jesus at Calvary can complete our desire for vengeance. We must remember what the Scriptures teach:

> *Dearly beloved, avenge not yourselves, but rather give place unto wrath: for it is written, Vengeance is mine; I will repay, saith the LORD.*
>
> Romans 12:19

> *For we know him that hath said, Vengeance belongeth unto me, I will recompense, saith the LORD. And again, The LORD shall judge his people.*
>
> Hebrews 10:30

It seems to me that we risk an unpleasant encounter with God when we seek to take vengeance into our own hands, for He has reserved vengeance as His own domain.

I have told many pastors that if they insist on releasing the angry and hateful emotions of their congregations, they had better keep a common enemy in front of their people, or angry parishioners will turn on them or on each other. This has proven true over and over again.

Whose war is this, anyway? According to the book

of Revelation, it is God's war. It is a conflict between angels:

> *And there was war in heaven: Michael and his angels fought against the dragon; and the dragon fought and his angels, And prevailed not; neither was their place found any more in heaven. And the great dragon was cast out, that old serpent, called the Devil, and Satan, which deceiveth the whole world: he was cast out into the earth, and his angels were cast out with him. And I heard a loud voice saying in heaven, Now is come salvation, and strength, and the kingdom of our God, and the power of his Christ: for the accuser of our brethren is cast down, which accused them before our God day and night.* Revelation 12:7-10

For those who take a futurist's view of this final book of the Bible, this conflict is yet to come. However, Jesus declared: *"I beheld Satan as lightning fall from heaven"* (Luke 10:18). If He saw it, it must have occurred already.

If this battle is yet to come, why was Satan allowed to tempt Jesus here on the Earth? What was the work of the cross? Not everything in the book of Revelation is awaiting future fulfillment. Much of the book is in the past tense or has a dual application.

This battle chronicled in Revelation took place aeons ago—long before the creation of human beings. It does not speak simply of a conflict between good and evil; it represents a contest of wills between God and Satan, God's avowed enemy.

Repeatedly (five times, according to Isaiah 14), Satan lifted his will above the will of Father God, and this became the basis for the conflict. Satan expressed a desire to have a position higher than that of God, and he is still working toward that same end.

The length of this continued conflict has led some to suggest a near equality of power and authority between God and Lucifer, but nothing could be further from the truth. God is the Creator, while Lucifer was the highest form of God's creation. That still makes him a creature. The length of the conflict does not suggest that God is incapable of bringing it to a conclusion. It suggests, rather, that He has chosen to use Satan as a means of testing His people and as a catalyst to drive us to the arms of Him Who created us.

We are children of God

It is not our assignment to destroy Satan, for God is not finished with him yet. As we will see in a later chapter, it is also foolish for us to step outside of our assigned role and to attempt to fill a role designed for another. Let God be God.

There are some Christian leaders now seen as specialists in this field of spiritual warfare. They travel from city to city to assemble Christians together for a good fight against Satan. It is Christ, however, Who is the Captain of God's army, not a man.

We must guard ourselves against those who would take a few portions of scripture out of context and use them to teach something that is clearly inconsistent with the rest of God's Word. Paul advised:

It's God's War

> *Study to show thyself approved unto God, a workman that needeth not to be ashamed, rightly dividing the word of truth.* 2 Timothy 2:15

If we are to remain free in God, we must compare scripture with scripture and principle with principle. Delightful as fresh inspiration may be, and as exciting as prophetic utterance may become, we must always judge both by the revelation of God's nature as given in the Bible, for God never contradicts Himself.

Whose war is it, anyway? While there can be no doubt that we need to recognize our enemy, know his territory and his strategy, know our weapons and learn to use them well and know how to get into the Spirit (for flesh and blood are of no value in spiritual conflicts), the Christian life is not nearly so complicated. Christ has paid the price for our salvation, and we must learn to appropriate His sacrifice and to glory in the finished work of salvation. Getting to know Him better is far more important than anything else we must learn.

Viewing the conflict of the last days, Daniel attested:

> *But the people who do know their God shall be strong, and do exploits.* Daniel 11:32

Why, then, are we putting such heavy emphasis upon knowing our enemy when the strong ones will be those who have experientially come to know their God? Is it easier to disseminate anger and hatred against Satan than to share the love and grace of Jesus?

No believer need be lost in this conflict. We can all remain at home, maintaining the family and home until the war is ended. Then, when our loving Bridegroom returns, we will have feasting and fellowship.

This is not our war, so we need not bring ourselves to spiritual exhaustion. Christ's Kingdom is a kingdom of peace and rest. His invitation, while He was here on Earth, was:

> *Come unto me, all ye that labour and are heavy laden, and I will give you rest. Take my yoke upon you, and learn of me; for I am meek and lowly in heart: and ye shall find rest unto your souls.*
>
> Matthew 11:28-29

Christ's promise was rest, not constant warfare. It was a relationship with Him in the yoke, not following behind Him in the infantry. He offers us His meekness, not His combativeness. And Christ does not force any of this upon us. The promise starts with, *"Come unto me."* Too many Christians are charging at the devil instead of coming to Jesus.

Recently the papers reported the good intentions of a man who stepped into a fight to separate the contestants. The two fighter men turned on the intruder, killed him, and then continued their fight. It doesn't always pay to intervene in another's fight.

God is more than a match for the devil. He doesn't need us to protect or deliver Him. By the word of His mouth, He created Satan, and by a spoken word, He will cast him into the Bottomless Pit. He will do all this in His time, however, not ours, and it is very likely that He will not need our help in doing it.

We are called to be congenial

Why is the church looking for a good fight? Is fighting more fulfilling than loving? Is hating Satan easier than loving God? Do we find it easier to fight an enemy we cannot see and do not even know—whether he is present or not—than to obey God who lives within us by the Holy Spirit?

Why are God's precious children playing with such costly and dangerous spiritual toys? May God's Spirit teach us the difference between war games in the backyard and obedience to God's Word in the everyday activities of life. If spiritual warfare as it is now commonly practiced by many is a game, then let's be honest enough to call it that.

If you strongly believe in spiritual warfare, please do not lay this book down now. Your continued spiritual existence may depend on the teaching that follows. Please be willing to look through my eyes for a few more pages. Let my more than sixty years in the ministry benefit your soul. The risk is too great to continue in this mock warfare without searching the Bible with understanding.

Are we victims of Satan? Not any longer. The psalmist of the Old Testament era felt that our victory was the result of the Lord's triumphant warfare, not ours. He wrote:

> *O sing unto the LORD a new song; for he hath done marvellous things: his right hand, and his holy arm, hath gotten him the victory.* Psalm 98:1

Paul did not see our victory as something we gain

through conflict, but as something we obtain through knowing Christ Jesus. If it is a gift, there is no need to strive for it; and if it is not a free gift of God, then His Word is in error.

John the Beloved did feel that there was an action needed on our part if we were to enter into full victory. He wrote:

> *For whatsoever is born of God overcometh the world: and this is the victory that overcometh the world, even our faith.* 1 John 5:4

The action God has required of every one of us is to believe in His finished work. The power of our faith is in its source—God. The value of our faith is determined by its object. If the faith we possess is a faith in our own ability to tear down enemy strongholds, it is of little value. If it is faith in our enemy, it will turn into fear and become a destructive force. If our faith is in God, that faith makes a complete cycle and brings into existence what God has promised.

God has promised us the victory. He has purchased that victory and He has proclaimed that victory throughout His Book. We must do little more than embrace that victory as ours and rejoice that the devil has nothing in us.

Whose war is it, anyway? Thank God, it's His.

CHAPTER 2

WHOSE DEVIL IS IT, ANYWAY?

Thou wast perfect in thy ways from the day that thou wast created, till iniquity was found in thee.
Ezekiel 28:15

Even in sports competition, knowledge of the opponent is vital. Football coaches diligently study video recordings of their adversary's games with other contenders. They want the edge of knowing how that competitor plays. If we dare to engage Satan in spiritual warfare, shouldn't we learn something about this dangerous enemy?

Paul declared:

Lest Satan should get an advantage of us: for we are not ignorant of his devices.
2 Corinthians 2:11

This does not suggest that we genetically acquire knowledge about the devil at conversion. Reading the Scriptures, observing life, and paying attention to the prompting of the Holy Spirit within our lives will give us the information we need about Satan. His devices have not changed since the creation of man. It should not be too difficult to spot them.

Some speak of Satan only as an evil influence and fail to recognize him as the highest of Heaven's creation. In far too many Christian circles, I observe an unfortunate confusion about the nature and work of the devil. Perhaps Christians have gained too many of their concepts of the devil from ancient Greek mythology and religious art. They characterize him as having horns, cloven hoofs, a forked tail and as running around in red underwear and using a pitchfork to prod Christians to try the pleasures of sin. This is an absolutely cunning deception.

Popular literature pictures the devil as a hopelessly vile being. Writers ask us to visualize the most debased person on Earth, and then tell us that Satan is a thousand times more vile. Often they project a picture of the degenerate drug addict or the perverted child molester and use this to describe the devil. If this is the "mug shot" you are carrying, I can assure you that you will not find the devil.

A third image of Satan that has again become popular pictures him as omnipresent (everywhere present) and omnipotent (all powerful). Those who support this view have reduced life to the dualism of the ancient Greeks that divorces men and women from any personal accountability for their actions. They place the Almighty in charge of all good, while Satan is in charge of all evil.

This view presents Satan as nearly equal in power with God and argues that since the conflict between right and wrong has raged for so many centuries, God and Satan must be equally matched, since neither has yet won the war. This has caused some individuals to embrace God theologically while serving the devil experientially. They want some insurance against the final outcome.

The fundamental error in this concept is the absence of the human will. The Bible does not teach dualism; it teaches a trinity of forces at work. There is the will of God, the will of Satan, and the powerful will of men and women, all operating concurrently. Submitting to the will of the devil is not the nucleus of sin. The prophet declared:

> *All we like sheep have gone astray; we have turned every one to his own way; and the* L*ORD* *has laid on him the iniquity of us all.* Isaiah 53:6

God's Word will not let us sidestep personal responsibility by crying, "The devil made me do it." Sin is a personal choice.

The Scriptures do not picture Satan as a vile being, as we consider vileness. He is consistently pictured as a very religious creature who understands worship better than we mortals do, for he was trained under the guidance of the Almighty God. In my book, *Worship As Jesus Taught It,* I say:

> *Satan is still far more interested in worship than in sin. He is more likely to be in church than in the worst den of iniquity in any area. This fallen angel would rather pervert a person's worship than corrupt his morals, for he knows that if he can pervert our worship, we will corrupt our morals.*

I am personally convinced that most Christians would not recognize the devil if he were seated next to them in church on Sunday morning. So how can we successfully fight an opponent we do not recognize?

Lucifer Exalted

I admit that the Bible does not tell us much about the one we call the devil. I am convinced, however, that we are told all we need to know about him. I cringe when I hear of Christians going to the occult world to see what those involved in such darkness have to say about Satan. Jesus told the religious leaders of His day:

> *Ye are of your father the devil, and the lusts of your father ye will do. He was a murderer from the beginning, and abode not in the truth, because there is no truth in him. When he speaketh a lie, he speaketh of his own: for he is a liar, and the father of it.*
>
> John 8:44

If Satan is an incurable liar, why should we pay any attention to what he says, even about himself?

We do not need to read books on Satanism to learn something of the nature of our enemy. God's Word gives us sufficient information about the devil. When we couple Isaiah 14 and Ezekiel 28 with Revelation 12, we get a fairly comprehensive picture of Satan. Ezekiel 28 describes this "being" as most glorious. We read: *"Thus saith the LORD GOD; thou sealest up the sum, full of wisdom, and perfect in beauty"* (verse 12). He was the capstone of God's creation. He was *"full of [God's] wis-*

dom" and absolutely *"perfect in beauty,"* as God counts beauty.

He was *"the anointed cherub that covereth"* (verse 14). In the Tabernacle in the Wilderness, this was represented on the lid of the Ark of the Covenant by two angels with outstretched wings protecting the holiness of God. God declared through the prophet, *"I have set thee so,"* so Satan held this exalted position by the choice of the Almighty.

God also tells us that Satan *"was upon the holy mountain of God...[and] walked up and down in the midst of the stones of fire"* (verse 14). His high rank among the angels brought him very close to the presence of God. His position in Heaven was near to the throne of God with all the privilege, prestige, and power that this position could provide. There was no created being in Heaven that had a higher position than him.

God also reminds him, and us, that Satan had dwelt in *"Eden the garden of God."* That was not Adam's Eden, but God's Eden. The paradise God prepared for Adam was only a scale model of the heavenly garden. Where the Genesis account says: *"And the LORD God planted a garden eastward in Eden; and there he put the man whom he had formed"* (Genesis 2:8), the Hebrew word translated "planted" literally means "transplanted." God brought plants from His Eden to Earth's Eden. Satan actually lived in God's private garden.

Through Ezekiel, God further informed us that the specific dwelling place of Satan was resplendently beautiful: *"every precious stone was thy covering"* (verse 13). Then it lists nine precious stones and gold as the materials used for his dwelling place.

God further informs us: *"the workmanship of thy tabrets and of thy pipes was prepared in thee in the day that thou was created"* (verse 13). Obviously, Satan was the first of God's creation with musical ability, which leads many to believe that he was in charge of the worship in Heaven.

From the general philosophy of the Scriptures, it seems that Satan, known in Heaven by the name Lucifer, was especially created with capacity to receive the energy of God's love and pass it on to the lesser angels, and then collect their returned love and give it to God.

Lucifer was second only to God in all of Heaven's creation. Furthermore, he seemed to have pleased God greatly, for we read: *"Thou wast perfect in thy ways from the day that thou wast created, till iniquity was found in thee."*

Since God created us *"a little lower than the angels"* (Psalm 8:5), we are no match for this highly exalted one. He is *"full of wisdom,"* while we only *"know in part."* He was *"perfect"* from the day of his creation, while we were *"born in sin and shapen in iniquity"* (Psalm 51:5). Satan lived in the garden of God, but we must wait for the day when we will be in God's recognized presence.

It seems obvious that Lucifer was made to serve God, not to serve us. He took His orders from the Almighty, not from lowly men and women. He is powerful; we are impotent. He is spirit; we are body, soul, and spirit. He comes from realms so far above us that Paul said:

> *Eye hath not seen, nor ear heard, neither have entered into the heart of man, the things which God hath prepared for them that love him.*
>
> 1 Corinthians 2:9

Isn't it dangerously presumptuous for us to attempt to enter the realm of Lucifer and struggle with him?

Lucifer Expelled

Of course, Satan is not now in the realms of God. He has been deported. Isaiah 14 tells us that this spiritual being embraced the possibility of replacing God in the heavens. God spoke about Lucifer to Isaiah:

> *How art thou fallen from heaven, O Lucifer, son of the morning! how art thou cut down to the ground, which didst weaken the nations! For thou hast said in thine heart, (1) I will ascend into heaven, (2) I will exalt my throne above the stars of God: (3) I will sit also upon the mount of the congregation, in the sides of the north: (4) I will ascend above the heights of the clouds; (5) I will be like the most High. Yet thou shalt be brought down to hell, to the sides of the pit.* Isaiah 14:12-15
> (parenthetical numbers added)

Not content with the exalted position God gave him, five times Lucifer exerted his will to be at least equal to God, if not replace Him. Of course this caused confusion in eternity, for until this moment there had been but one will in all of God's creation—His own. Now there were two wills, and the angels were faced with the decision to choose sides between Almighty God and Lucifer, the pretender prince. If this same force did not work in our own natures, we would never understand this rebellion, but the same spirit is at work in all of us.

Because of his strong lusting to receive the adulation of the angels for himself, rather than gathering it to present it to God, Lucifer rebelled and had to be cast out of Heaven. We have no indication in Scripture how lengthy this process of self-exaltation may have been, but the very fact that he could exercise this volition five times before God took radical action is an indication of God's gracious nature.

While Isaiah tells us that Lucifer was cast down from Heaven, it is the book of Revelation that better describes the action. With His amazing ability to condense, the Holy Spirit uses but three verses to describe this major conflict:

> *And there was war in heaven: Michael and his angels fought against the dragon; and the dragon fought and his angels, And prevailed not, neither was their place found any more in heaven. And the great dragon was cast out, that old serpent, called the Devil, and Satan, which deceiveth the whole world: he was cast out into the earth, and his angels were cast out with him.* Revelation 12:7-9

The Bible gives us no actual description of the action. It lists only the results of the war. We are informed that the conflict was not between Jehovah and Lucifer. God knew it would be far too unmatched a battle for the Creator to fight against His creation, so He chose to let a high-ranking angel fight against an even higher-ranking angel. God commissioned an archangel, Michael, to throw Lucifer and his army out of Heaven. Armed with God's spoken word, Michael was completely successful in casting Lucifer from his high position close to the throne of God.

Although we have no knowledge about the actual battle, we do know that only two things changed. First, God changed Lucifer's name. The Bible no longer calls him by his heavenly name, Lucifer. According to Revelation 12:9, it calls him:

1) Serpent
2) Dragon
3) Devil
4) Satan
5) Deceiver

These are all descriptive nicknames for the one who was second only to the Godhead itself. Both the words "devil" and "satan" mean *deceiver*. Three times God warns us of the deceptive tactics of this great being by saddling him with names that scream his nature to us every time we speak them.

The second change that came out of Heaven's war was Lucifer's position. In his expulsion, Lucifer came to this Earth. We do not know whether this was by his choice or by God's decree. The book of Revelation would suggest that Satan still has access to Heaven, but only as an *"accuser of the brethren"* (Revelation 12:10).

What did not change was Satan's desire to replace God. He still wants to place his throne higher than the throne of God. He is a very religious being who desires, and probably needs, praise and worship. His goal on Earth is far less the destruction of mankind than it is to receive worship from men and women who were created to give their worship to God. This is the true evil in his nature.

Satan exposed himself in his temptation of Jesus by seeking to get the Christ of God to worship him. Christ's answer was to quote the Old Testament:

> *Jesus answered and said unto him, Get thee behind me, Satan; for it is written, Thou shalt worship the* LORD *thy God, and him only shalt thou serve.*
>
> Luke 4:8
>
> (see Deuteronomy 6:13-14)

The object of worship became the motivation for the conflict. This was Satan's original desire, and it remains unchanged to this day.

THE DEVIL AS AN EXECUTIVE

The war in Heaven was not between two angels; it was between two divisions of Heaven's angels. We read: *"Michael and his angels fought...and the dragon fought and his angels"* (Revelation 12:7). We also read: *"His angels were cast out with him"* (Revelation 12:9). Since the fourth verse of this chapter tells us, *"His tail drew the third part of the stars of heaven, and did cast them to the earth,"* most Bible scholars teach that Lucifer brought a third of Heaven's angels with him. This would be consistent with the concept of the early Christian church that since only three angels are named—Michael, Gabriel, and Lucifer—all three were archangels with one third of Heaven under their respective control.

Lucifer was a leader in Heaven, and he remains a leader on Earth. He had angels under his jurisdiction in Heaven, and he has them under his command on Earth. He has organized and arranged his kingdom on Earth the way God has His Kingdom ordered in Heaven. Why not? After all, everything Satan knows he learned in Heaven. There is no scriptural indication that Satan has creative powers or original thoughts; he is preprogrammed.

In his letter to the Colossian Christians, Paul described the progressive order of God's Kingdom as being fivefold:

> *For by (1) him were all things created, that are in heaven, and that are in earth, visible and invisible, whether they be (2) thrones, or (3) dominions, or (4) principalities, or (5) powers: all things were created by him, and for him.* Colossians 1:16
> (parenthetical numbers added)

With Almighty God at the head, His Kingdom has five levels. It is interesting that when Paul warned the Ephesian Christians about the devil's kingdom, he also listed four levels beneath the devil. He wrote:

> *For we wrestle not against flesh and blood, but against (1) principalities, against (2) powers, against the (3) rulers of the darkness of this world, against (4) spiritual wickedness in high places.*
> Ephesians 6:12
> (parenthetical numbers added)

The devil is not everywhere present, but he has agents of his demonic world working for him throughout the entire Earth. They are not equal in authority or ability. Although the ultimate responsibility for their actions is charged to Satan, he operates much as the head of a worldwide corporation.

It is a serious mistake, then, to call every level of this kingdom "the devil." Perhaps some of the opposition believers experience is the work of the devil, but most of it is not the devil personified; it is the devil portrayed by a lower level of his kingdom. When we scathingly denounce the shipping clerk in the name of the president of the corporation, we not only make ourselves look ridiculous; we are totally ineffective in producing results.

The Devil Expurgated

Looking to the future for what is available in our present denies us present enjoyment and postpones prevailing victories. Somehow the victory of Christ's cross has escaped many believers. They look forward to the time when Jesus will ultimately defeat the devil, while the New Testament affirms that Christ's cry from the cross, *"It is finished,"* was provisionally the end of Satan's kingdom. Just as with every other aspect of the cross, victory over Satan remains only for us to appropriate.

At Christ's ascension, He paused at Satan's headquarters to strip him of all rank, position, authority, and power. Paul declared this:

> *And having spoiled principalities and powers, he made a show of them openly, triumphing over them in it.* Colossians 2:15

The Greek word here translated as "spoiled" is *apekduomai,* which literally means "to divest wholly; to despoil." It is a military term that is used nowhere else in the New Testament. Paul chose this word with full knowledge of its meaning and implication. He was familiar with the ways of the Roman army. In my book, *Let Us See Jesus,* I wrote:

> *When a Roman general finally conquered his foe, especially if the battle had been long and especially hard fought, the official surrender often became a formal, full-dress affair with the two leaders facing each other in the presence of their respective armies. After the signing of such documents of surrender as might have been drawn up, the conqueror stepped up to the defeated general, who stood at rigid attention in his full dress military uniform with all insignias, medals, badges, and other symbols of position and authority that pertained to his position of leadership.*
>
> *Systematically, the conqueror stripped these symbols off the uniform of the defeated general to the accompaniment of beating drums. When every symbol of power, position, rank, and honor had been forcibly ripped from the uniform, the Roman general would announce, "Now all of these are mine by right of conquest. What you were, I now am. The titles you held, I now hold. Your armies will now obey me, and your nation will forever be subject to the rule of Rome.*
>
> *This ritual was called* apekduomai. *Movie goers and TV viewers will recognize the ceremony from*

western scenes in which an officer of the cavalry was disgracefully stripped of his rank and drummed out of the service.

It was with full understanding of this ceremony that Paul declared that at the time of Christ's Ascension, He divested Satan of every position of authority and every vestige of power that God had ever given him before his expulsion from Heaven.

What a scene that must have been! Jesus, pausing in His Ascension through the satanic kingdom to call for a full-dress parade, demanded that Satan stand at attention in full-dress uniform. Jesus stepped before him and, in a voice that rang clear into the corridors of Hell, declared:

"Now is come salvation, and strength, and the kingdom of our God, and the power of his Christ: for the accuser of our brethren is cast down, which accused them before our God day and night." *Revelation 12:10*

Reaching to the right epaulet of Satan's uniform, Jesus stripped it off, saying: "You were created Lucifer, which means 'day star' *(see Isaiah 14:12). I hereby strip that title from you forever, for I shall be known as* 'the bright and morning star' *" (Revelation 22:16). Transferring this to His left hand, Jesus reached for the left epaulet and jerked it off the uniform, saying. "You held the position of the* 'anointed cherub' *(Ezekiel 28:14), but I now have the title of the* 'Anointed One' *" (see Acts 10:38).*

Turning to His attending angel, Jesus directed that these epaulets be placed on the display table in full sight of the entire forces of Hell.

Fixing His fingers on the gold braid of Satan's uniform, Jesus stripped it off in one quick action and said: "You have functioned as the 'tempter' (see Mark 1:13), but from now on I will be a 'guide' *(see Isaiah 58:11) to mankind."*

Focusing His attention on the many medals Satan wore, Jesus began to strip them off the uniform one by one, authoritatively declaring: "I saw you as lightning falling (see Luke 10:18), but men shall see Me as lightning that shineth from the east to the west" (see Matthew 24:27). You were the first creature of God's creation in which music was expressed (see Ezekiel 28:13), but from now on 'In the midst of the church will I sing praise' *(Hebrews 2:12). You have been an effective* 'hinderer' *(see 1 Thessalonians 2:18), but I will be a* 'helper' *(see Psalm 63:7). You have been that* 'old serpent' *(Revelation 12:9 and 20:2), but I am as the serpent that was lifted up for men's healing (see John 3:14). You have been an* 'adversary' *to My people (1 Peter 5:8), but I'm now their* 'advocate' *(1 John 2:1). You have functioned as an* 'angel of light' *(2 Corinthians 11:14), but* 'I am the light of the world' *(John 8:12). You have been the* 'accuser of the brethren' *(see Revelation 12:10), but I am now their* 'Counsellor' " *(Isaiah 9:6).*

With this, Jesus paused to place all these stripped medals into the care of the angel, who spread them out on the table to the side of Satan and Jesus. Both the armies of Heaven and Hell watched as Jesus reached for the five stars on the uniform of Satan. "I hereby strip you of your title of 'prince of this world' *(John 14:30) and declare that I am both a* 'Prince and a Savior' *(Acts 5:31); I am the* 'Prince of Life' *(Acts 3:15), and I am the* 'KING OF KINGS AND LORD OF LORDS' " *(Revelation 19:16).*

At this declaration the armies of Heaven could restrain themselves no longer. In an excited cadence they cried:

"Alleluia; Salvation, and glory, and honour, and power, unto the Lord our God. For true and righteous are his judgments." *Revelation 19:1-2*

Waiting for this demonstration to end, Jesus looked Satan coldly in the eyes and, without blinking an eyelid, reached for the stars on the other collar, declaring, "You were created as one of the sons of God (Job 1:6), but I am 'The Son of God' *(Mark 1:1 and John 1:18, emphasis added). You have lost everything my Father gave to you; they are now My possessions."*

Stripped, humiliated, and divested of all authority, Satan had to remain at attention while Jesus lifted these various symbols of position and rank in full sight of Hell's armies. In the relieved voice of a conqueror, Jesus told them, "Satan and his entire kingdom are defeated. All his power has been stripped from him. His authority has been transferred back to Me, and his kingdoms are now My kingdoms. You will henceforth be under the rule of the Heavenly Kingdom. Bounds and limits will be set upon your activities beyond which you will not dare to go. Failure to comply means you will have to deal with Me. I am your God, and you will obey Me."

> *At the sound of this proclamation, the anger, frustration, and incredulity that had characterized the attitude of Hell's legions gave way to fear. They cowed, turned their heads, trembled, and some even collapsed in their ranks. There was no doubt in my mind that Jesus Christ had fully conquered them—once and for all.*
>
> *Gathering all of these tattered remnants of Satan's power and authority, Jesus completed His Ascension into the heavens where He put them in a display case for all of Heaven's inhabitants to see. Every angel in the eternal abode knows that Satan has been completely stripped—*apekduomai. *Both Heaven and Hell know that Satan is merely a figurehead, a puppet, an exile. It is only mankind who seems unaware that the "*roaring lion*" (1 Peter 5:8) has had his teeth pulled and is on a leash to the "*Lion of the tribe of Judah*" (Revelation 5:5). The only power left to him is the power of persuasion, but this was all that he needed in the Garden of Eden to "con" man into departing from God's control to his own. Oh, that God could cause today's Church to examine the display case containing these trophies of Christ's victory over Satan!*
>
> (*Let Us See Jesus,* pages 87-91)

Whose devil is it? Indisputably he belongs to God. God created him, exalted him, expelled him, and has now expurgated him. When God no longer needs his service, He will intern the devil in the Lake of Fire.

If we have occasion against the devil, we should deal

with his boss—Jehovah God—rather than deal directly with the enemy. Just as I have no right to fire another man's employee, no matter how he or she may have mistreated me, so I have no right to order Satan around. He is not my employee; He belongs to God.

Chapter 3

Whose Captain Is It, Anyway?

And he said, Nay; but as captain of the host of the LORD *am I now come. And Joshua fell on his face to the earth, and did worship, and said unto him, What saith my lord unto his servant?* Joshua 5:14

Many preachers use the book of Joshua and compare his conquest of the Promised Land to our conquest of Satan and his kingdom. There are some beautiful parallels between these battles and our battles with self and sin, but I question whether it is sound exegesis to compare the Promised Land with the kingdom of Satan. I have also heard many speakers compare the Promised Land with Heaven by making it the antithesis of the wilderness, which they refer to as our present earthly experience.

Personally, I am not interested in possessing Satan's kingdom, for God has promised me a place in His Kingdom, and it is far superior to anything I could take away from the devil. I also consider it to be a mistake to compare the Promised Land with Heaven. The Heaven I am going to is not filled with enemy usurpers. Heaven is the abode of God, and I don't see Satan abiding in the presence of God after his expulsion from Heaven.

If, as I will suggest later in the book, the conquest of the land of promise pictures the struggle that goes on in the minds of believers, then the method of conquest is definitely worth a closer look.

In reading the book of Joshua, I see Joshua's meeting with the Captain of the Host of the Lord as pivotal. If Joshua had missed this encounter, it is unlikely that he would have succeeded in his invasion. The limited military experience he and his soldiers possessed was totally insufficient for the conflict that lay before them. While it is true that we learn by doing, Joshua could have lost his entire army during the learning process.

Just as the Bible records the war in Heaven in a mere three verses, this confrontation between Joshua and Jesus also requires only three verses:

> *It came to pass, when Joshua was by Jericho, that he lifted up his eyes and looked, and, behold, there stood a man over against him with his sword drawn in his hand: and Joshua went unto him, and said unto him, Art thou for us, or for our adversaries? And he said, Nay; but as Captain of the host of the* L*ORD* *am I now come. And Joshua fell on his face to the earth, and did worship, and said unto him, What saith my lord unto his servant? And the Captain of the* L*ORD*'*s host said unto Joshua, Loose thy shoe from off thy foot; for the place whereon thou standest is holy. And Joshua did so.*
>
> Joshua 5:13-15

To understand this passage, six questions need to be answered:

1. What was Joshua doing?
2. What was Joshua seeing?

3. What were Joshua's questions?
4. To whom was Joshua speaking?
5. What was Joshua's posture?
6. What instructions were given to Joshua?

If we are to place ourselves in Joshua's position as mighty conquerors, we should be willing to face these same six questions before the battle begins.

What are we doing?

Every person God has ever called to service was doing something. God uses busy people. He calls those who have learned the discipline of productive activity, and Joshua was such a person. He had been a faithful attendant to Moses for forty or more years, until the responsibility of leadership of all Israel fell on his shoulders at Moses' death.

Joshua, chosen by God to conquer the Promised Land, was not a young, inexperienced man. God wisely chooses mature men and women to lead His people in conflicts. While we must admire the zeal of young leaders, we have every reason to question their wisdom.

When the mourning period for Moses had ended, the LORD spoke to Joshua, giving him some specific commands. Before Joshua met Jesus, God tested his obedience level. First, God told him to lead the people across the flooded Jordan River. The method he was to use was different from the way Moses had led his people through the Red Sea, for Joshua's faith must be in the living God, not in a method of operation.

It is always easy for us to embrace the patterns of the

past as guidelines for the future instead of listening to the voice of God for today. God may not want us to do what Moses did. He wants us to do what He says to us today.

Secondly, God gave Joshua very explicit instructions about how to bring the Ark of the Covenant into the new territory. The Ark symbolized God's presence among His people, and Jehovah wanted that presence to become a part of the new experience. We may move from the wilderness into the Promised Land, but we dare not move from the presence of God.

Joshua next obeyed the Lord in circumcising all the men of Israel. The people who came out of Egypt entered into covenant with God through circumcision, but they did not bring their children into this covenant. As those who had entered covenant with God died in the wilderness, it left only those who had benefitted from the covenant, without having ever personally cut covenant with God. God insists that those who enter battle with Him must be in an intimate covenant relationship with Him. The posture of Joshua was: no covenant commitment, no battle, and no inheritance.

Joshua also caused the people to observe the Passover and led them in eating the corn of the land instead of remaining dependent upon the manna that had sustained them in the wilderness.

After all this, Joshua brought the army to Jericho—the first enemy to be conquered. He was now ready to face his first great fight.

We can answer the question, "What was Joshua doing?" by simply saying that he was doing the most recent thing God told him to do. God wants obedience to His word far more than He wants ingenuity or sacrifice. To Saul, Israel's first king, God said:

> *Behold, to obey is better than sacrifice, and to hearken than the fat of rams.* 1 Samuel 15:22

Whatever else Joshua may have been, he was an obedient servant of God. He had learned in service under Moses that until we have done what God has requested, He will give us no further orders. How easy it is to substitute service—even sacrificial service—for obedience to the known will of God! Sometimes we would rather volunteer to fight the devil with others than to spend private time with God in prayer. Shouting the devil out of the heavens, however, is no substitute for reading God's Word until His truth penetrates our hearts and minds.

Almost all of us prefer to be involved in something big than in something small. The bigness of the idea of challenging the satanic realm may seem more fascinating than the work God has called us to:

> *Casting down imaginations, and every high thing that exalteth itself against the knowledge of God, and bringing into captivity every thought to the obedience of Christ.* 2 Corinthians 10:5

It has been my observation through some sixty years in the ministry that most Christians choose whom they want to obey and in what particulars. God wants immediate and implicit obedience to what He has said, and He is not interested in our substitutions.

What are we seeing?

This must have been a very insecure time for Joshua. The children of Israel were on enemy territory, no longer in the wilderness. The encampment of God's people no longer enjoyed the visible symbol of God's presence in the cloud and the pillar of fire, nor did they have access to the daily manna. That had all ceased when they crossed the Jordan River.

Everything was different and new, and both are fear producing. Add to this the discomfort of newly circumcised men, and it is difficult to paint a rosy picture of the military encampment close to Jericho. Although spies had reported that the inhabitants of Jericho were terrified of the Israelites, that terror was based on reports of what God had done more than forty years before. That had been another time and another generation. This generation was born in the wilderness and had not seen the miracles of Egypt or the parting of the Red Sea.

Seeking the slice of seclusion that leaders often need, Joshua left the camp and walked toward Jericho. He probably wanted to see this fortified city for himself, for it had been more than forty years since he and Caleb had spied out this territory.

There was plenty to occupy Joshua's attention. He could have studied the walls of Jericho, or he could have looked back at his meager encampment. He could easily have looked introspectively inward, but Joshua made a right decision:

> *He lifted up his eyes and looked, and, behold, there stood a man over against him with his sword drawn in his hand.* Joshua 5:13

Joshua neither looked out nor in; he looked up. He did not need to assess the enemy's strength further or reassess his personal weakness; he needed a greater glimpse of God. He looked up, and God accommodated him with a comforting revelation of Himself—as the Captain of the Host of the Lord.

The psalmist knew the value of lifting his eyes to the Lord, for he wrote:

> *Unto thee lift I up mine eyes, O thou that dwellest in the heavens. Behold, as the eyes of servants look unto the hand of their masters, and as the eyes of a maiden unto the hand of her mistress; so our eyes wait upon the* L*ORD our God, until that he have mercy upon us.*
>
> Psalm 123:1-2

Joshua could have stared at Jericho until fear overwhelmed him. He could have scrutinized his own forces until he was in despair. Instead, he chose to look upward toward his God, and God comforted him.

What are we looking at when we come together to do battle against Satan? Most exhortations at these moments seem to be more about the devil than about Jesus. Most prayers are directed at the devil, as we tell him what to do and when to do it. The energy of the congregation is directed toward the negative force of the devil rather than the positive force of Jesus Christ. The tragedy of this is that we are apt to see what we are looking for.

In my first book, *Let Us Praise,* I tell how the congregation I pastored in Eugene, Oregon, was experiencing demonic oppression and bondage in its services. It seemed necessary for me to step to the pulpit, address the demons, and command them to leave before we could have liberty in praise and worship.

One Monday in my prayer room, the Lord told me He would like to have top billing in our church instead of letting Satan have it. I protested that Jesus was, indeed, number one with us. He told me that recently I never led the congregation into worship of Himself before I had exalted demons. I was totally taken aback by this thought, but He explained that recognizing the presence of demons, calling them by name, and telling them what I expected them to do (flee) all exalted them and actually constituted "worship" in the demonic realm.

It broke my heart to realize I had unwittingly been leading my congregation into the exaltation of demons. When I asked the Lord what I should do, He sweetly told me to just lead the congregation in praising Him, and He would take care of the demonic activity among us. I did that, and He did what He had promised. We never again called attention to a demon in a public service.

We must all learn to look upward. In the early days of the Charismatic movement, we saw Jesus in every service. How is it that this got turned around, and many people began seeing demons every time they gathered together? Has our attention been diverted from the One we have gathered to worship? May God redirect our gaze until we, too, can declare:

> *We see Jesus, who was made a little lower than the angels...crowned with glory and honour.*
>
> Hebrews 2:9

What are our questions?

The Scriptures tell us that when Joshua saw *"A man over against him with his sword drawn in his hand,"* he *"went unto him, and said unto him, Art thou for us, or for our adversaries?"* (Joshua 5:13). Joshua had probing questions. They were important questions, for the action he was to take depended upon the answers he got to his questions. In simple terms, Joshua asked, "Are you friend or foe?"

The LORD's resounding "No!" to Joshua's question, "Are you for us or for our adversaries?" has always delighted me. The LORD had come to be Himself, not to be on someone's side. It is human to declare that God is for us, but against "them." Armies have gone to war convinced that God was on their side. Athletes have testified to their invincibility, because God was with them. Even church congregations have predicted their success and the doom of other churches because, they said, "God is on our side." God does not take sides with men and women; He calls men and women to get on His side.

God does not love the saints and hate the sinners. John the beloved declared:

> *For God so loved the world, that he gave his only begotten Son, that whosoever believeth in him should not perish, but have everlasting life.* John 3:16

Joshua learned from God's "No!" that the issue was not what side God had placed Himself on. The higher issue was whether Joshua, through obedience, would be on God's side.

This is a desperate need within the fellowship of believers to learn that God is not automatically on our side. We do not have the option to do what seems right, assuming that God will make it all work out. What we need to learn is how to get on God's side—how to join Him in what He is doing, instead of trying to coerce God to join us in our activities.

Many of us talk to God as if He is duty bound to do exactly what we tell Him, as if we expect Him to leave His heavenly throne to come to Earth and play toy soldiers with us. The New King James translation of Psalm 115:3 reads: *"But our God is in heaven; He does whatever He pleases."* We must learn what His pleasure is instead of continually informing Him of our desires.

Joshua wanted to know whether he was dealing with friend or foe. Often we have been found contending with God because we saw what He was doing as the work of our adversary. We also fail to see that we are our own worst enemy and must struggle against our own flesh. God is never our adversary; He is always for us. Much of the time, we are the real enemy. Jesus said:

> *For out of the heart proceed evil thoughts, murders, adulteries, fornications, thefts, false witness, blasphemies.* Matthew 15:19

We consistently place the battlefield outside of ourselves, but the Bible insists that the conflict is within. We would rather battle Satan in the sky than sin in the mind. This, however, is the real battlefield.

Many years ago the classic Christian writer, C.S. Lewis, wrote a book titled *Your Devil Is Too Big, and Your God Is Too Small.* The book is a challenge to allow God to be to us who and what He declares Himself to be, and it had a profound influence upon my life when I first read it.

We must learn how to get on God's side, to accept Him for who He says He is, to abandon the lie of the supremacy of Satan and to embrace the revelation of the invincibility of our God. Perhaps we, like Joshua, need to call on God asking, "Who are You?" When we do it, He will answer us.

Who is this being?

While Joshua was seeking to know whose side this Mighty One was on, the Lord was trying to tell His servant who He was. He said to Joshua: *"As captain of the host of the LORD am I now come"* (Joshua 5:14). Some want to know whose side God is on, and others want to know what God can do for us, but what God wants to do is to reveal Himself to us. He is not anxious that we know His methods or His plans, as much as He is that we know *Him.*

How sad that we seldom want what God wants! Paul's secret of success in ministry was knowing the Lord. He wrote:

> *I know whom I have believed, and am persuaded that he is able to keep that which I have committed unto him against that day.* 2 Timothy 1:12

The source of Paul's confidence and faith was his personal knowledge of God. He knew who Jesus was. He had seen Him, he had talked with Him, and he was aware that Christ lived in him through the Holy Spirit. We need this experiential knowledge if we are to be successful in warfare against sin.

Who was this person Joshua saw with the unsheathed sword? His own declaration was: *"As captain of the host of the LORD am I now come."* He introduced Himself as the leader of Heaven's armies.

This phrase, *"LORD of hosts"* occurs in two hundred and seventy-three verses of scripture. When the psalmists used it, they usually sang, *"LORD God of hosts."* The prophet Isaiah used the term more than fifty times, while Jeremiah used it more than eighty times. Often the term was used to describe the one speaking: *"Thus saith the LORD of hosts"* (Jeremiah 51:58).

Every time the Old Testament used this phrase, our translators capitalize the word LORD, showing that it signified Jehovah God. Most Bible scholars see this as a manifestation of Jesus, for when He was on the Earth, He was called LORD.

This *"Captain of the host of the LORD"* was none other than Jesus Christ Himself, coming among His people in the form of a man to lead them into triumphant victory. He did not come, however, to lead an army of men. He came to lead the hosts of Heaven. The book of Hebrews speaks clearly of Jesus, when it says:

> *For it became him, for whom are all things, and by whom are all things, in bringing many sons unto glory, to make the captain of their salvation perfect through sufferings.* Hebrews 2:10

Jehovah God chose to make Jesus Christ *"the captain of [our] salvation."* He is the Savior, and we are the saved.

He is the Captain, and we are the ones rescued from the imprisonment of the enemy.

That Jesus was fully aware of His position as Captain over all of Heaven's host of warrior angels is evident in the Garden of Gethsemane. When Peter ineffectively used his sword and cut off the ear of a servant of the high priest, Jesus told him:

> *Thinkest thou that I cannot now pray to my Father, and he shall presently give me more than twelve legions of angels?* Matthew 26:53

As Captain (or, as we would say today, Commander-in-Chief) of Heaven's armies, Jesus had a vast array of heavenly forces available to Him, and He still does.

This role of Captain or leader of Heaven's armies has never been given to men. It is a title and office reserved exclusively for Jesus. Any person who presents himself or herself as our deliverer, protector, or the Captain of God's armies is a usurper or a pretender. Those who claim an ability to command Heaven's angels are deluded. Those angels are God's angels, and they take their orders directly from Jesus. They will no more follow our instructions than friendly soldiers would take orders from an opposing general.

We must meet the true Captain, just as Joshua did, and until we do, we will follow pretenders and fall into defeat with them.

What is our posture?

When the Captain disclosed His role to Israel's leader, Joshua's response was moving. He *"fell on his face to the earth, and did worship"* (Joshua 5:14). Joshua had stood face to face in equality with this Captain, but once he knew Who this was, he immediately prostrated himself. This was none other than God manifested.

Bowing in this way is the posture of surrender. Joshua could not have made himself more vulnerable to the Man with the drawn sword. With his face in the dust, he could not even see what the Man was doing, much less be able to defend himself against an attack. He put himself entirely at the mercy of the Lord.

The first step in true spiritual warfare is to make ourselves vulnerable to God. We may assume that the sword of truth in the hand of God is against our enemies, when it may, in reality, be used against us. We need the cutting edge of divine truth to prune wild branches from our lives. If we are inadvertently walking in error, we need to bow before the sword of the Word and allow it to cut out the delusion and replace it with truth.

By prostrating himself before the Captain, Joshua made himself available to whatever this heavenly being had been sent to do. Jesus did a similar thing in the Garden of Gethsemane:

> *And he went a little farther, and fell on his face, and prayed, saying, O my Father, if it be possible, let this cup pass from me: nevertheless not as I will, but as thou wilt.* Matthew 26:39

It is not in the exercising of our wills that spiritual victories are won; it is in the surrendering of our wills to the will of God. The Spirit cannot accomplish much in our lives as long as we have a feeling of equality with

God. There comes a time when each of us must bow in humility before God to receive whatever He chooses to do in us.

When Joshua fell on his face before this Captain, he worshiped, and worship is true spiritual warfare. In worship, we are giving glory, honor, exultation, and adulation to the One who has obtained our victory. All our energy is being directed to Him, none of it toward Satan. As we worship the Lord, heavenly hosts are at work defeating the enemy. Our role is to worship; the angels' role is to carry out the battle in the heavenlies. We rejoice in the Lord while they resist the demon forces.

Quality spiritual warfare is apt to be done on our knees, while our faces are prostrate on the floor, or when our spirits are raised to God above. We must remember the scriptural admonition:

> *Submit yourselves therefore to God. Resist the devil, and he will flee from you.* James 4:7

Submission to God must preface resistance of the devil. Actually, it is this submission to God that provides a means of resistance to the devil, for we are yielding our lives to the One who has completely defeated the evil one.

Abasement always precedes battle. This is why we put servicemen through boot camp. No commander wants to enter a conflict with men whose wills have not yet been brought to instant obedience. The chain of command must be ingrained in the recruit. Don't be one of those who insist on skipping God's boot camp.

What instructions are given?

Following his worship, Joshua asked this Captain: *"What saith my lord unto his servant?"* (Joshua 5:14). Under Moses, Joshua had been the second in command for more than forty years. He was promoted to the number one position only at the death of Moses, and he met the Captain about two months later. His first response was to surrender his position of leadership and ask for orders. From this moment on, Joshua was again the second man, and during the entire conquest of Canaan, he took orders from his Captain.

Joshua was not deactivated; he was just repositioned. He was still commander of Israel's army, but he took his orders from the Captain of Heaven's army. God has no desire to deactivate us either, but He does want to reposition us. We are not to act until He tells us what to do, when to do it, and how to do it.

It is interesting to note the one instruction the Captain of Heaven's hosts gave to Joshua upon that first meeting:

> *Loose thy shoe from off thy foot; for the place whereon thou standest is holy. And Joshua did so.*
>
> Joshua 5.15

Although the land that Joshua stood on was enemy territory, the presence of the Captain made it holy. Even when we are on demonic territory, if we are aware of the divine presence, the place where we find ourselves is holy ground. Wherever our holy God is present, that place becomes holy. How much better it is, then, to worship Him than to direct our energies at the enemy.

The request that Joshua remove his shoes is reminiscent of the ancient custom pictured in the book of Ruth. When Boaz wanted to redeem the property of Naomi and take Ruth for his bride, he recognized that there was an heir one step closer than himself. It would be necessary for this man to relinquish his rights to the claim before Boaz could redeem it. In the presence of ten elders of the city, Boaz asked the kinsman to redeem the land. His response was:

> *I cannot redeem it for myself, lest I mar mine own inheritance: redeem thou my right to thyself; for I cannot redeem it. Now this was the manner in former time in Israel concerning redeeming and concerning changing, for to confirm all things; a man plucked off his shoe, and gave it to his neighbour: and this was a testimony in Israel. Therefore the kinsman said unto Boaz, Buy it for thee. So he drew off his shoe.*
>
> Ruth 4:6-8

This Captain asked Joshua to admit that he could not redeem the land that God had given to Abraham, but which had been lost when the children of Israel went into Egypt. He asked for the one with the right of redemption to take off his shoes as a legal symbol of transferring those rights.

The heart of spiritual warfare is taking off our shoes and giving them to Jesus. We cannot bring redemption, but we can surrender our legal claim to Him who is able, and surrendering our claim allows Him to do what He is fully able to do.

As long as we are trying to defeat the devil, the Lord

refrains from intervening on our behalf, but when we surrender our rights in a display of inability, He quickly redeems for us everything that sin has wrested from us. Removing our shoes of authority at the feet of the Master will do far more than stomping them in an attempt to defeat the devil. If we will worship God, He will to the work.

Joshua was not given any further instructions. He was in a right posture, he was asking the correct questions, and he was doing the right thing. All further information was given to him as he needed it, and so it is with us. God does not reveal His complete plan to us at one time. He gives us orders as they are needed. When we obey what He says—removing our shoes in humility before Him—He will continue to speak to us and reveal His will to us.

CHAPTER 4

WHOSE KINGDOM IS IT, ANYWAY?

> *Jesus went about all Galilee, teaching in their synagogues, and preaching the gospel of the kingdom, and healing all manner of sickness and all manner of disease among the people.* Matthew 4:23

The gospel book that connects the Old Testament with the New says this of Jesus. Matthew, a former tax agent, used four active verbs to describe the ministry of Jesus. He said that Jesus went, Jesus taught, Jesus preached, and Jesus healed. He further defined this action by telling us where Jesus went, where exactly He taught, what He preached, and who He healed. While we now have libraries of books telling us the details of what Jesus preached, those who walked with Him consistently reduced the subject of Christ's preaching to one simple phrase. He preached, they said, "the kingdom of God" or "the kingdom of Heaven."

Jesus did not seem to know that Satan was in charge of everything. No one told Him that Satan had wrestled this world from the Father's control. He also paid little attention to the political jurisdiction of Rome or the religious authority of the high priest. Just as the president of the United States need not pay undue attention to the mayor of a local town, so Jesus knew His jurisdictional rights as King of kings and Lord of lords.

Jesus seemed assured that wherever the King walked, the Kingdom was manifested. His presence brought the Kingdom to Earth just as His presence secured the Kingdom in Heaven. The true issue is not the locale, but the personnel. Where Jesus is, the Kingdom of Heaven is revealed.

To a subjugated and oppressed people, Jesus happily proclaimed:

> *Repent: for the kingdom of heaven is at hand.*
> Matthew 4:17

Jesus never spoke of having to take the Kingdom back from Rome, religion, or the satanic realm. He simply called for a personal turning from sin to enter the Kingdom of Heaven that He declared was then present.

Much of Christ's teaching concerned the Kingdom of God. For Him, it was not a subtheme; it was His main theme. He mentioned the Kingdom fifty-five times in the Gospel of Matthew. The four gospels speak of the Kingdom more than one hundred and twenty-five times. Even after His resurrection, Jesus spent forty days with His disciples, *"speaking of the things pertaining to the kingdom of God"* (Acts 1:3).

In the Sermon on the Mount, Jesus began by saying:

> *Blessed are the poor in spirit: for theirs is the kingdom of heaven.* Matthew 5:3

What follows is a list of the governing rules for the attitudes of Kingdom dwellers. Some have called them "the be attitudes." Christ made no attempt to amass an army of believers to wrestle the Kingdom from the hand of the enemy. He simply proclaimed that the Kingdom was now, and this is the way to function in it.

Toward the end of Christ's ministry, He turned His attention from the multitudes and ministered to His disciples. The turning point is seen in Matthew 13 where He preached a series of parables to a multitude so vast that He had to use a boat for His pulpit. When the disciples asked why He spoke to the people in parables, Jesus said:

> *In them is fulfilled the prophecy of Esaias, which saith, By hearing ye shall hear, and shall not understand; and seeing ye shall see, and shall not perceive: For this people's heart is waxed gross, and their ears are dull of hearing, and their eyes they have closed; lest at any time they should see with their eyes and hear with their ears, and should understand with their heart, and should be converted, and I should heal them. But blessed are your eyes, for they see: and your ears, for they hear.*
>
> Matthew 13:14-16

In these parables, Jesus used seven similes for the Kingdom of Heaven. He said that the Kingdom was like:

1. A sower (verse 24)
2. A mustard seed (verse 31)
3. Leaven (verse 33)
4. Hidden treasure (verse 44)
5. A merchant man (verse 45)

6. A net (verse 47)
7. A householder (verse 52)

When He spoke of the Kingdom of Heaven, Jesus avoided spiritual jargon and used the language of laymen. He used illustrations of His Kingdom that were so plain and practical that common people could easily relate to them. He did not speak of the Kingdom as futuristic, but as current and present.

Christ consistently considered the Kingdom as His. He embraced His legal rights to every facet of that Kingdom. He demonstrated His kingly authority over the elements of the Earth by walking on water, calming a storm, and multiplying bread and fish. He proved His authority over Satan in the temptation in the wilderness, and He repeatedly forced demons to obey Him. He healed every form of sickness, restored life to the dead, and forgave men and women their sins.

Who dares say that Satan is the king over this world? He is a usurper prince who only manipulates control whenever sinful people will submit to him.

The Kingdom is God's by right of creation

From the first chapter of the Bible, God teaches us that He is the Author of all existence. God's Book begins:

> *In the beginning God created the heaven and the earth.* Genesis 1:1

We see a personal God calling into existence by the

exercise of His almighty will things that had not been. He manifested this will by expressing His Word, and He executed that Word by His Spirit.

Since the Hebrew word for God here in Genesis is *Elohim*, a plural form of the word "God," it was not God the Father in the act of creation, but God the Father, God the Son, and God the Holy Spirit bringing forth something out of absolutely nothing. In the prologue to his Gospel, John wrote:

> *In the beginning was the Word, and the Word was with God, and the Word was God. The same was in the beginning with God. All things were made by him; and without him was not any thing made that was made.* John 1:1-3

The rest of this chapter establishes conclusively that this Word (Logos) was indeed Jesus. While it is true that creation can be ascribed to God the Father (as it is in Romans 11:36), it is equally true that God never acts independently; He always acts through the agency of the Son. The Bible is very explicit on this subject:

> *All things were made by him; and without him was not any thing made that was made.* John 1:3

> *[God] hath in these last days spoken unto us by his Son, ...by whom also he made the worlds.*
> Hebrews 1:2

> *For by him were all things created.*
> Colossians 1:16

By virtue of His relationship to God, Christ is the ground of Creation, both in Heaven and on Earth, and He is simultaneously its means and its end. Christ Jesus is, therefore, supreme over the universe. To underscore this, Paul lists four pairs of divisions in the universe:

> *(1) Heaven and earth; (2) visible and invisible; (3) thrones or dominions, or (4) principalities or power: all things were created by him, and for him.*
>
> Colossians 1:16
> (parenthetical numbers added)

God, in Christ Jesus, created all spheres, whether in the heavens above or the Earth beneath. There is no locality that He did not bring into existence. Beyond that, He created the nature of all things—some visible and some invisible. Furthermore, He created all the inhabitants in those spheres, whether thrones, lordships, principalities or dominions. Paul affirms that the invisible beings of the world above us, however lofty their names or mighty their powers, are His creatures as much as the lowest objects within our sight.

Because the invisible world is such an unknown to us, Paul uses two pairs of descriptions where the first is greater than the second—*"thrones or dominions, principalities or powers."* It is presently impossible for us to know fully what these terms convey concerning the various hierarchies of Heaven, for the Scriptures have not given us much understanding of that glorious realm, but they do seem to point to gradations of being and to distinctions of official glory.

Still, all these invisible beings, so illustrious as to be

seated on thrones, so great as to be called *"dominions,"* so exalted as to be considered *"principalities,"* so potent as to merit the designation of *"powers,"* were created by the Son of God, and they all acknowledge His supremacy and glory. The highest position in creation is infinitely below Him, and there is neither majesty nor renown that equals Him. Not only were all things created by Him, *"All things were created...FOR Him"* (Colossians 1:16, emphasis added).

Apart from Christ, there would have been no Creation at all. He was the reason for it. He was the First Cause and the Final Cause, the Alpha and the Omega of Creation. This world, with its forests, mountains, lakes, and flowing meadow streams, with all its flowers, fruits, birds, and butterflies, was made so beautiful because it was Christ's world.

Other worlds, peopled by the heavenly hosts, were also created, that His glory might be revealed to and through them as well. It is an unscriptural philosophy that teaches that all things were made for man, for even man himself was created unto Christ's glory (see Ephesians 1:12). Christ Jesus, not man, is the great end of Creation. As surely as all Creation emanated from Him, so it all converges again toward Him.

There can be no doubt that Heaven was created for Him, for it is the place of His special residence and the future home of the redeemed. Obviously the angels were created for Jesus, for they are messengers of His mercy, executors of His will, and executioners of His vengeance. Equally, Hell was created for Jesus, for it is the prison of His justice. Even the Earth was created for Him, for it was the scene of His incarnation and atoning death, and is the seat of His mediatorial Kingdom.

Furthermore, the human race was created for Christ Jesus, for man was created in His image and is recreated into that image through the new birth. To the church in Corinth, Paul quoted the psalmist when he wrote: *"For the earth is the LORD's and the fulness thereof"* (1 Corinthians 10:26), but David had added, *"the world, and they that dwell therein"* (Psalm 24:1).

Jesus is not only the purpose of creation, He is also the perpetrator of all creation. We read: *"By Him all things consist"* (Colossians 1:17). J.B. Phillips translates this verse: *"He is both the first principle and the upholding principle of the whole scheme of creation."*

Jesus is the Conserver as well as the Creator of all things. Apart from Him, atomic fission would explode the universe into fragments. If it were not for Jesus, all things would fall asunder and go back into nothingness. All the laws of the universe that regulate and give stability to matter subsist in Christ and are nonexistent outside of Him.

The universe found its completion in Jesus and is sustained and preserved every moment by the continuous exercise of His almighty power. All things hang on Christ. If He withdrew His upholding hand, everything would run into confusion and ruin. He is the center of life, force, motion, and rest; around Him all things revolve. He imposes their limits, gives to them their law, strikes the keynote of their harmonies, and blends and controls their diverse operation, for He is the All-perfect in the midst of imperfection, and the Unchangeable in the midst of change.

The Bible never says this about Satan. He is not a

creator; he is a created being. He even lacks the power of procreation that God has given to men and women.

THE KINGDOM IS GOD'S BY REASON OF RESERVATION

I have heard preachers enthusiastically declare that God turned the rulership of this world over to Adam when He created man and woman and placed them in Eden. Then these preachers declare that the purpose of the temptation in the Garden of Eden was to wrest this control from Adam's hands and give the dominion of this world unto Satan. This philosophy does not fit the Genesis record. There is not the slightest hint in Genesis that God gave the dominion of this world to Adam. What we read is:

> *And God said, Let us make man in our image, after our likeness: and let them have dominion over the fish of the sea, and over the fowl of the air, and over the cattle, and over all the earth, and over every creeping thing that creepeth upon the earth.*
>
> Genesis 1:26

This is repeated two verses later when God told Adam and Eve to *"be fruitful"* and to *"replenish the earth."* God did not give men and women full authority over His creation. Man was only given dominion over some of God's creatures—fish, fowls, cattle, and creeping things.

God is a perfect Father. He, far better than we, knows how dangerous it would be to put all creation into the hands of His fledgling children. Like the wealthy parent whose last will and testament provides for a limited income for the children until they reach maturity, so God gives only as much authority as He feels His children can handle and increases that dominion as they mature.

Adam had much to learn, and God was his only teacher. Maturing was a long process for him. When Satan approached him in the garden, Adam's only dominion was over the garden and the living creatures in it. He was the gardener and zoologist of Eden. He was not in control of the Earth, much less the master of the universe, as some suggest.

There is nothing in the temptation of Satan that suggests he thought he could wrestle the Earth away from Adam and Eve. His goal was to take Adam and Eve away from God. His allure was to cause this first couple to disobey God, for Satan knew this would cut them off from their Creator. Satan's conflict was with God, not with Adam. He worked on our first parents to hurt God.

Adam was but the gardener in God's garden. If, as some project, Satan did wrest from Adam the control and authority God had given to him, then Satan must tend God's garden and exercise control over God's animals. As gardener, he is limited to pulling weeds, for Jesus said:

> *Every plant, which my heavenly Father hath not planted, shall be rooted up.* Matthew 15:13

Satan can neither sow nor plant in God's garden without knowing that everything he plants will be weeded out. It is still God's garden, and He chooses what will remain and what will be removed. This is still God's world by right of His reservation. He deliberately chose to limit the authority He gave to men and women. The psalmist declared:

> *Thy kingdom is an everlasting kingdom, and thy dominion endureth throughout all generations.*
> Psalm 145:13

God did not hand the Kingdom over to Adam. His dominion endures throughout all generations because He did not consign it to Adam and his progeny.

Satan would like to delude us into believing that this world is his domain and that he has authority here, but this is a loud bluff. David assured us:

> *The kingdom is the LORD's: and he is the governor among the nations.* Psalm 22:28

Satan is but a squatter. He doesn't own one square inch of this Earth. He has no power beyond what God has given to him, and that power is conferred and can be withdrawn at any time.

THE KINGDOM IS GOD'S BY RIGHT OF REDEMPTION

Because of Adam's sin, the entire Earth came under the curse of sin. God told Adam, *"Cursed is the ground for thy sake"* (Genesis 3:17). What all this entails is beyond our grasp, for we have but a fleeting glimpse into what this creation was like before this curse was pronounced. It seems likely that more than *terra firma* was included in the curse.

The theme of the Bible is God's redemption from sin. It began in the garden with the substitutionary death of animals so their skins could form clothes to cover the nakedness of Adam and Eve. This redemption was completed at Calvary when Jesus cried from the cross, *"It is finished"* (John 19:30). We no longer live with a covering to hide our sins. We are cleansed from the presence, pollution, power, and penalty of sin. The promise is:

> *If we walk in the light, as he is in the light, we have fellowship one with another, and the blood of Jesus Christ his Son cleanseth us from all sin.*
>
> 1 John 1:7

Paul extends this redemptive work to all of God's creation. He wrote:

> *Because the creature itself also shall be delivered from the bondage of corruption into the glorious liberty of the children of God. For we know that the whole creation groaneth and travaileth in pain together until now.* Romans 8:21-22

This world is God's by right of creation and by right of redemption. Even the beasts God put under the care of Adam belonged to the Lord. Asaph the psalmist reminds us:

> *Every beast of the forest is mine, and the cattle upon a thousand hills.* Psalm 50:10

Redemption brings back something that was forfeited. When we say that the earthly realm belongs to God by right of redemption, we do not mean that God lost it, or pawned it, and now He is buying it back. God never lost man or the Earth, but man, through sin, lost his contact with God. Redemption is for man's sake. Even the redemption of this Earth is for the sake of glorified men and women.

Redemption is a process of reconciliation. The Scriptures never speak of God being reconciled to men and women; it is always men and women being reconciled to God. Similarly, it is always people and things being redeemed, never God being redeemed. The process of redemption is God's creation being restored to its original purpose, and the Redeemer is the Possessor.

How could Satan gain control of a kingdom that God has redeemed? Had God abandoned it, we might say that the squatter gained possession by default, but God has never abandoned His world. He has maintained an active interest in it from the day of creation until now.

Where did the devil get enough power or cunning to sneak this world out of the control of God? He didn't. He couldn't. He is too far beneath God to ever outmaneuver the Almighty. All projections that this is the devil's world must come out of observing what unredeemed men and women have done to the world, not from the pages of the Bible.

Why is it that when various groups of Christians gather together, all they seem to see are demons? They look to the sky above them and see it full of devils. David looked to the sky and sang:

> *The heavens declare the glory of God; and the firmament showeth his handiwork.* Psalm 19:1

Another psalmist declared:

> *The heavens declare his righteousness, and all the people see his glory.* Psalm 97:6

These writers of Israel's song book also saw the Earth as filled with God's goodness, not the devil's power. They wrote:

> *The earth is full of the goodness of the* LORD. Psalm 33:5

> *The earth is full of thy riches.* Psalm 104:24

> *The earth, O* LORD, *is full of thy mercy.* Psalm 119:64

Lest we see these statements as little more than poetic license, may I remind you that when Isaiah looked into Heaven and saw the Lord sitting upon His throne, he heard the seraphim chanting: *"Holy, holy, holy, is the* LORD *of hosts: the whole earth is full of his glory"* (Isaiah 6:3). The Bible declares that the Earth is full of God's goodness, riches, mercy, and glory. How can we dare say that it is only full of demonic wickedness? Where is the eye of faith that sees what God sees?

The Kingdom is God's by right of declaration

It is possible to lose control by maintaining silence.

Just as a private road can become a public thoroughfare through neglect of posting it and occasionally closing it, so the usurper prince could end up in control of this earthly kingdom if God maintained silence. However, God has not been mute about this issue. He has repeatedly declared His ownership, authority, and rulership of this domain. Listening to Israel's anointed and inspired singers, we hear:

> *For the kingdom is the* LORD*'s: and he is the governor among the nations.* Psalm 22:28

> *The* LORD *hath prepared his throne in the heavens; and his kingdom ruleth over all.* Psalm 103:19

> *Thy kingdom is an everlasting kingdom, and thy dominion endureth throughout all generations.*
> Psalm 145:13

These men lived in a day of gory hand-to-hand combat. They suffered with pestilence and drought, and they lived under the heavy hand of an absolute monarchy. Still they did not see demons behind every bush. They knew by revelation of the Spirit of God that they lived in a kingdom ruled by Almighty God, and God the Holy Spirit proclaimed this truth through their lips.

The Spirit not only sang through these men of God's authority and rulership in this earthly realm, but through the prophets God loudly declared:

> *Saviours shall come up on mount Zion to judge the mount of Esau; and the kingdom shall be the* LORD*'s.*
> Obadiah 1:21

Of the increase of his government and peace there shall be no end, upon the throne of David, and upon his kingdom, to order it, and to establish it with judgment and with justice from henceforth even for ever. The zeal of the L*ORD of hosts will perform this.*
Isaiah 9:7

In the closing years of Paul's life, while he lived under house arrest in Rome, the Spirit proclaimed the Kingdom of God in the very seat of world government. We read:

Paul dwelt two whole years in his own hired house, and received all that came in unto him, Preaching the kingdom of God, and teaching those things which concern the Lord Jesus Christ, with all confidence, no man forbidding him. Acts 28:30-31

Of all the great doctrinal truths Paul wrote, the Spirit moved upon him in his final years to emphasize preaching the reality of Christ's Kingdom.

Perhaps the most positive declaration of Christ's Kingdom on Earth comes to us in the final book of the Bible where we read:

There were great voices in heaven, saying, The kingdoms of this world are become the kingdoms of our L*ORD, and of his Christ, and he shall reign for ever and ever.* Revelation 11:15

It is important to notice the tense of the verb used here. The declaration is present tense, not future tense.

They *"are become,"* or as other translators put it, *"have become."* Christ reigns in the present. This is His world right now. He has provisionally conquered every foe and has redeemed this world back to Himself.

I am not unaware of the political, religious, and spiritual kingdoms functioning here on Earth, but I am aware that they exist only by the mercy of God. Some day all kingdoms other than the Kingdom of Christ will crumble and lay at His feet like ashes. In Heaven, where time is nonexistent, this submission of all earthly kingdoms is seen as a present reality. In our time dimension we still wait for the fulfillment of what Heaven sees as accomplished.

Jesus reigns; the devil rants. Christ has conquered; the devil is the conquered one. This is God's world; the devil merely squats in a vacant building. Should we expend our spiritual energies trying to evict such a squatter, when we could be worshiping and adoring the One Who is in complete control of everything on this Earth? When the Lord needs the building where Satan is squatting, he will be evicted and placed on hold in the bottomless pit for a thousand years.

Those who believe that this is the devil's world have bought a lie. It simply is not so. He may be its occupant, but he is certainly not its owner.

CHAPTER 5

WHOSE ARMY IS IT, ANYWAY?

> *The* LORD *shall utter his voice before his army: for his camp is very great: for he is strong that executeth his word: for the day of the* LORD *is great and very terrible; and who can abide it?* Joel 2:11

Jesus wisely told His disciples: *"Ye shall hear of wars and rumors of wars: see that ye be not troubled: for all these things must come to pass, but the end is not yet"* (Matthew 24:6). Mark turned this last phrase to say *"For such things must needs be"* (Mark 13:7). Did Jesus mean that wars are a divine decree that must be carried out? I seriously doubt this. With the vision of a prophet and the hindsight of a sage, He was merely emphasizing that human nature without the working of the Holy Spirit is given to conflict, contention, confrontation, and combat. The heart of sin is an insistence upon having one's own way. This self-will caused Satan's expulsion from Heaven, Adam's eviction from Eden, and our exile from peace.

Unfortunately, dissension, disagreement, and discord are not the exclusive attributes of the unsaved. They are native to our human natures. Christian believers are capable of conflict too. Just look at the many church splits that have occurred in recent years.

God created us to be ruled, but we want to be rulers. He designed us to love, but we are inherently given to hatred. From the days of Cain and Abel, it takes very little jealousy or pride to produce a fight to the end between brothers and sisters. This is not a modern phenomenon. Nearly two thousand years ago, Paul reported:

> *For it hath been declared unto me of you, my brethren, by them which are of the house of Chloe, that there are contentions among you. Now this I say, that every one of you saith, I am of Paul, and I of Apollos; and I of Cephas, and I of Christ.*
> 1 Corinthians 1:11-12

The Corinthians were dividing themselves into different armies. The members of each unit took the name of the person under whom they had been converted. The saints in Corinth, however, did not have a monopoly on this type of attitude. James asked the believers to whom he wrote:

> *From whence come wars and fightings among you? come they not hence, even of your lusts that war in your members?* James 4:1

While Paul pointed out the problem, James pointed to the root cause—uncontrolled lust. Lust for possessions, for protection, for power or pride are at the heart of all personal wars.

Jesus said that there would be *"wars and rumors of wars"* until He returned, and history proves the accuracy of this prediction.

Whose Army Is It, Anyway?

One of the first actions of a new ruler is to form an army. Why? Armies are for conquest, for defense and for control, but they have often been used for nothing more than ego building.

From antiquity, men have used armed might to wrest territory from others in a survival of the fittest. Right of ownership surrenders to might of opposition, with the conquered usually becoming the slaves of the conquerors.

Why are Christians trying to invade enemy territory? Do we actually want Satan's kingdom or are we anxious to undo his works and release his prisoners? We must not rush into battle without advanced thought. Jesus observed:

> *Or what king, going to make war against another king, sitteth not down first, and consulteth whether he be able with ten thousand to meet him that cometh against him with twenty thousand? Or else, while the other is yet a great way off, he sendeth an ambassage, and desireth conditions of peace.*
>
> Luke 14:31-32

It is unwise to begin a war you know you cannot win, and it is equally inadvisable to attack an enemy whose strength is unknown.

The second reason armies are amassed is for defense. Since conquest is common, we often feel that we must be prepared to fight to maintain possession of our territory and goods. Is this the reason for amassing armies of Christian believers for warfare against Satan?

If spiritual warfare is for defense, what are we defending? Surely we aren't defending God, for He needs no defense. If we are defending ourselves, we have taken over the work of angels (as we will see in the next chapter). We need never defend our salvation or anything God has done in, for, or through us. David taught us that God is our defense. He likened God to about every defensive mode that he understood. He sang, *"My defence is of God, which saveth the upright in heart"* (Psalm 7:10).

The third reason for armed conflict is to control others. The Soviet communists were adept at using armies to control their populations, but when communism collapsed, civil wars soon broke out, and many nations seceded, causing a disintegration of the Soviet Union.

Are Christians coming together in great armed camps to try to keep the devil under control? Whose devil is he, anyway? It is unlikely that our feeble human efforts could exert much control over a creature such as Satan. God has permitted him to be free for a purpose.

The fourth reason for arming is for ego building. Leaders of nations have sacrificed the lives of millions of young men just to build their egos. As Napoleon Bonaparte said: "Soldiers usually win the battles and generals get the credit for them." Could it be possible that one motivation behind the popularity of spiritual warfare could be ego building for the leaders involved?

God used armies of men for natural conquest

God often used armies of men for divine purposes. The conquest of the Promised Land is a good case in point. Under God's direction, Joshua engaged and defeated the armies of the seven nations who inhabited the land that God had given to Abraham.

God could have used other means, but He didn't. He had the plagues in hand, but He didn't use them. He could have stirred one nation against another, as He often did later, but on this occasion He chose not to do it that way. One good pestilence could have destroyed the enemy squatters, but God chose to use the army under Joshua's command. Why? Perhaps God felt that by participating in the conflict, the people of Israel would develop a deeper appreciation for the land. Maybe their need to fight for the land was a transition from the relative inactivity of the wilderness to the hard physical work necessary in an agriculture society. Whatever reason God had, His Captain directed Joshua and the army in the conquest of the land.

A similar pattern was revealed with David. Repeatedly God used David's armies to subdue neighboring nations. He was even able to do what Samson was commissioned to do, but never accomplished—subdue the Philistines.

David never hesitated to ask God's counsel in battle. If God's word came to him through a prophet or a priest, David obeyed it instantly. Sometimes what God said kept David out of battle and, at other times, it delayed the battle. God frequently altered David's battle plans. As long as David obeyed the Lord, he was victorious.

Since both Joshua and David were godly men in leadership over Israel, we could expect God to use their armies. It is more difficult to realize that God has also used the armies of unbelievers. Nebuchadnezzar is an obvious example. He was the world conqueror who built the Babylonian Empire. He was an egomaniac who came under the judgment of God for his great pride and his failure to realize that God had allowed, and even helped him, in building his great kingdom.

Nebuchadnezzar was also the king whom God used to defeat Judah and to destroy Jerusalem. After the fall of the sacred city, God told the prophet:

> *And now have I given all these lands into the hand of Nebuchadnezzar the king of Babylon, my servant; and the beasts of the field have I given him also to serve him. And all nations shall serve him, and his son, and his son's son, until the very time of his land come: and then many nations and great kings shall serve themselves of him.* Jeremiah 27:6-7

God actually called this heathen king *"my servant,"* and rewarded him for his service. Nebuchadnezzar's armies became the armies of God, fulfilling His will and purpose.

There is no reason to believe that this ceased with the rise of modern civilization. The Seven-Day War in Israel seemed to include divine intervention. God used Israel's army to maintain the independence of that nation.

This is God's world, and its kingdoms are under His ultimate control. The psalmist declared:

> *For promotion cometh neither from the east, nor from the west, nor from the south. But God is the judge: he putteth down one, and setteth up another.*
> Psalm 75:6-7

God can use the scepter of death to shift power from one person to another, or He can use contesting armies to achieve it.

Many of the recent books about spiritual warfare point to biblical battles where God fought through earthly armies as models for spiritual warfare. I am aware of what Paul taught the Corinthians about examples given for our admonition:

> *These things happened unto them for ensamples: and they are written for our admonition, upon whom the ends of the world are come.*
>
> 1 Corinthians 10:11

Examples, however, are not necessarily patterns. Perhaps if we were part of an earthly army, fighting a human enemy, we might find more pattern in these Old Testament examples of God's utilization of Joshua's army. Spiritual warfare, however, is not a physical conflict using armed men in combat, and it is dangerous to take natural methods into a spiritual conflict. Jesus warned us:

> *It is the spirit that quickeneth; the flesh profiteth nothing: the words that I speak unto you, they are spirit, and they are life.* John 6:63

Because we know so little about our own spirits, to say nothing about the spirit world, it seems foolish to seek to engage spiritual forces with fleshly weapons and human methods.

There are glorious principles we can gain from studying the battles fought by Joshua and David, but their military tactics and methods of combat will not work for spiritual warfare. Ours is a very different enemy. Our weapons are extremely dissimilar to their weapons. In contesting spiritual forces, God uses spiritual beings and, at best, we are only one-third spirit.

God has armies of angels for spiritual conquest

Heaven has its own army, which the Scriptures call *"the heavenly host."* Luke wrote of *"a multitude of the heavenly host"* (Luke 2:13). These heavenly beings were present to protect Jesus at His birth. We would expect God to have a fighting unit among His angels, for Lucifer, the highest ranking angel the Almighty ever created, rebelled against God in an attempt to replace Him.

As we saw earlier in Chapter 2, this perpetrated a war in Heaven:

> *There was war in heaven: Michael and his angels fought against the dragon; and the dragon fought and his angels, And prevailed not; neither was their place found any more in heaven.*
>
> Revelation 12:7-8

This was a battle between high-level spirit beings, a battle between the will of God and the will of Lucifer. The weapons used were words, and God's word prevailed, as it always will. Michael merely applied the word of God against the will of Lucifer and cast the dragon (as he is called in this passage) out of Heaven.

When Jesus resisted the temptation of Satan in the

wilderness, His answer to each temptation was, *"It is written."* Satan used words or ideas as his weapon against Jesus, and Jesus used words as His weapon against the enemy. Because Jesus used the words of God, He prevailed. When this massive temptation was over, we read:

> *Then the devil leaveth him, and, behold, angels came and ministered unto him.* Matthew 4:11

It was not that the angels arrived just as Jesus finished the fight. They had been there all the time, and when their enemy retreated, they ministered to the physical weakness of Jesus.

As we saw in Chapter 3, Jesus is the Captain, the Commander-in-Chief, of Heaven's army. He defines the enemy, He determines the strategy, and He leads the battle. No wonder Heaven's army never loses! The prophet Joel declared: *"The LORD shall utter his voice before his army: for his camp is very great: for he is strong that executeth his word: for the day of the LORD is great and very terrible; and who can abide it?"* God's army is voice-controlled, and it is powerfully equipped to execute every command of Christ. Joel was convinced that nothing and no one could successfully resist the Lord's army. This spiritual army recaptures any territory Satan may have seized. For instance, the Bible tell us that Satan is:

> *The prince of the power of the air, the spirit that now worketh in the children of disobedience.*
> Ephesians 2:2

I believe that after he was cast out of Heaven, Satan set up his kingdom in the atmosphere of this world in an attempt to place his authority between God and the Earth. This allows him to be more than *"the accuser of the brethren"* (Revelation 12:10). He has also become an interference to the brethren. He seeks to hinder our access to God and God's access to us.

When Philip introduced Nathanael to Jesus, Nathanael marveled that Jesus had seen him sitting under a fig tree in a vision. Jesus said to him:

> *Because I said unto thee, I saw thee under the fig tree, believest thou? thou shalt see greater things than these. ... Verily, verily, I say unto you, Hereafter ye shall see heaven open, and the angels of God ascending and descending upon the Son of man.*
>
> John 1:50-51

Jesus was telling this disciple that at His ascension He would burn a pathway between Earth and Heaven and would become Jacob's ladder for New Testament saints. Jesus conquered territory that was once held by Satan. He keeps it secure with His presence so that nothing can hinder our prayers from ascending to God, and nothing can restrict God's answer to those prayers from getting to us. This is spiritual warfare that only Jesus could successfully wage.

The Bible does not say how many angels Jesus used in this battle, but it does say that He won gloriously. We do not need to burn a hole through Satan's kingdom, as some would suggest. Jesus has already made a secure route through the demonic realm into the divine Kingdom.

Another Bible evidence of warring angels comes from the book of Daniel. This prophet, who held high political office in Babylon, set his heart to seek the Lord. After a three-week complete fast, Daniel was given a vision that exhausted all his strength. When a mighty angel was sent to strengthen Daniel, he said:

> *Fear not, Daniel: for from the first day that thou didst set thine heart to understand, and to chasten thyself before thy God, thy words were heard, and I am come for thy words. But the prince of the kingdom of Persia withstood me one and twenty days: but, lo, Michael, one of the chief princes, came to help me; and I remained there with the kings of Persia.* Daniel 10:12-13

Nothing had prevented Daniel's prayer from getting to Heaven, but there was an angelic conflict that hindered the special-delivery answer God sent. When the angel seemed unable to break the power of the Prince of Persia, God dispatched Michael to assist His heavenly messenger. Before leaving Daniel, this great angel confided in him:

> *Now will I return to fight with the prince of Persia: and when I am gone forth, lo, the prince of Grecia shall come.* Daniel 10:20

The angel had experienced conflict both coming and going, but no matter how powerful the Prince of Persia may have been, it took only this angel and Michael to defeat him. Heaven's army is always victorious.

This is God's army, and it is under God's control. We do not have a place in it, nor has God given us a voice in its command. God fights these spiritual battles with spirit beings. Flesh and blood cannot participate in this warfare. Our part is to conduct the cheering section, filling the atmosphere with praise and worship.

GOD DOES NOT CALL HIS CHURCH AN ARMY

For many years I have resisted the idea that we humans are part of God's literal army. I don't even like military-type hymns. While I agree that we are soldiers in God's army as a simile, I feel that it is too often projected as actual fact. When Ezekiel spoke of the resurrected dry bones as *"an exceeding great army"* (Ezekiel 37:10), it was an obvious comparison, not a declaration of fact.

Paul called for us to put on the full armor of a soldier (see Ephesians 6). He also reminded Timothy:

> *No man that warreth entangleth himself with the affairs of this life; that he may please him who hath chosen him to be a soldier.* 2 Timothy 2:4

Both of these statements are comparative, and neither of them makes a Christian a soldier in a literal army. The Christian life does call for defensive armor, and it calls for disengagement from the world, but I am sure that the true meaning of these passages is much deeper. We will discuss this issue in greater detail in a later chapter.

If I am wrong and the Church is God's army on

Earth, may God help us! Today's Church hasn't even learned to stand in rank. When we are issued a spiritual weapon, we tend to destroy one another with it. We are so carnal that we don't even know our true enemy, so we fight anything that moves or is different from ourselves.

If the Church is God's army, we don't stand a chance in the battle against Satan. We are only one-third spirit, while Satan is all spirit. We don't know where he is and only have an awareness of him when some member of his kingdom assaults us. Our whole approach to this warfare is defensive. We are like a blind man trying to fight off a street gang. We flail our canes and scream a lot, but we cannot defend ourselves, much less launch an offensive attack against our tormentors.

If the Church is God's army, why is disobedience so rampant in the ranks? Has anyone been through boot camp? I don't see the instant obedience to God's chain of command that is essential to successful warfare. The church obeys out of emotion rather than out of dedication. Even most of the giving in our churches is motivated by appeal rather than divine command.

If the Church is God's army, who is in command? Prayer is unpopular in the church, and I get the impression that few preachers and even fewer laymen spend much time in God's presence. How do we know what we are supposed to do in this army if we never talk with headquarters?

No, the Church on Earth is not God's literal army. The Bible speaks of believers as the Bride of Christ. I have often said that I do not wear combat boots; I wear bedroom slippers. I am a lover, not a combat soldier.

God did not redeem me to place me in a combat division of His army. He saved me out of love, and He calls me His Bride. When war breaks out, it is better that I stay at home and wait for His return. Nothing hinders a battle more than having wives out in the crossfire of the battlefield.

The Bible calls us the family of God. We are in a filial relationship with one another, not in a military affiliation. God has called us to love, sustain, and care for one another as a large family. Christ has not placed us side by side in the trenches; He has brought us into the Father's house to enjoy His love and provision and to interact with one another.

There is not the slightest hint in Scripture that the underlying motivation for redemption is to give God a greater army with which to fight the devil. God is not short-staffed in His army. If God requires a greater army, He need but speak the creative word and have thousands of angels standing at attention to do His bidding.

We have been redeemed unto God; not unto the army. We have been rescued from the kingdom of Satan, not called to destroy his kingdom. Christ commissioned us to be bearers of the good news that Christ has come, not heralds that the army has arrived in a declared war. Ours is a ministry of healing, not a ministry of destruction. We have the role of saviors in this world, not soldiers.

Many like to play army

Why are many in the Church so fascinated with warfare? Do we prefer to pull down rather than build up? This may reflect the spirit of our age. In our cities, gangs of youth systematically burn, pillage, or tear down what someone else has built or gathered. It takes little knowledge to destroy, whereas building requires maturity. Perhaps we Christians are too immature and frustrated to be constructive, so we resort to being destructive.

Previous generations knew little of the ravages of war unless the war was on their territory. That is no longer true. Television brings war into our living rooms, although it may be occurring on the other side of the world. We visualize the carnage, the suffering, and the destruction. Why would we choose this as the model for our Christian gatherings?

About ten years ago, I was a guest speaker in a church in Northern Ireland. We were near Belfast—the very heart of the conflict between the Protestants and the Catholics. The services were held in a public building that was also the meeting place for a segment of one branch of the army. The pastor was leading his congregation in "spiritual warfare" and used military commands and marches and led his congregation in chanting Christian war songs.

I asked him, "Is it really safe to present the Gospel in a military fashion when mere identification with the Christian army is an invitation for a terrorist attack from the Catholics?"

He responded, "I had never thought of that. I just wanted to defeat the devil."

"Jesus defeated the devil at Calvary," I told him. "This charade you are playing with your congregation is putting them at risk needlessly."

That was the end of playing soldier for that pastor. I wish other pastors could see the futility of their war games. We don't pull down the enemy; we often destroy people's faith. We don't edify the believers with our games; we often lead them into deception. As Arthur Ponsonby said years ago: "When war is declared, truth is the first casualty."

John Abbott wrote: "War is the science of destruction." The heart of war is to kill. The winner is usually the army that has more men left than the other army. Has Christ commissioned His Church to kill or to make alive? Jesus said:

> *The thief cometh not, but for to steal, and to kill, and to destroy: I am come that they might have life, and that they might have it more abundantly.*
> John 10:10

> *I am the light of the world: he that followeth me shall not walk in darkness, but shall have the light of life.* John 8:12

If Christ came to give life, where did the Church get the commission to kill and destroy? Jesus said this was the mission of the thief.

I know the argument leaders give for this type of spiritual warfare is that we are only destroying the enemy, but, as Jawaharlal Nehru of India observed, "It is the habit of every aggressor nation to claim that it is acting on the defensive."

Possibly many in the Church are enamored with warfare because we would rather conquer than possess. Perhaps we feel it is easier to take away than to maintain. War may seem easier than living a Christ-centered life in the community and the home. The Church of this generation seems to want what the world possesses and is willing to fight to gain it. While it appears that we are fighting the devil, it usually ends in earthy rewards. Who is kidding whom?

Maybe we would rather steal members of other churches as prisoners of war than to produce new converts. In all major wars, prisoners are put to work as slave labor as replacements for the workers who went to war. Religion has often followed this pattern of enslavement of persons instead of bringing them into spiritual liberty in Christ Jesus. Some leaders refuse to help others grow up and keep them dependent for job security and even prostitute them financially and morally for the benefit of the leader. These become war casualties. They are victims of friendly fire.

Harry Emerson Fosdick said, "The tragedy of war is that it uses man's best to do man's worst." This becomes the sad condition in the groups that concentrate on warfare. We use God's glorious gifts to do our worst, for we direct it to the devil instead of to God.

Probably the greatest tragedy of our mock war games is that we fail to fill our true God-given roles in this world, as we shall see in the next chapter.

Chapter 6

Whose Role Is It, Anyway?

All things are of God, who hath reconciled us to himself by Jesus Christ, and hath given to us the ministry of reconciliation; To wit, that God was in Christ, reconciling the world unto himself, not imputing their trespasses unto them; and hath committed unto us the word of reconciliation.

2 Corinthians 5:18-19

After an extensive period of ministry in Germany and England several years ago, I flew into Sky Harbor Airport in Phoenix. Since my wife had caught the flu, my brother Robert volunteered to meet me and drive me home. On the drive home, I shared with him the commission I had just received to write this book and he said, "I have some material you can use, but it will cost you a hundred copies of the book."

"Let's hear it," I said. "If I can use it, you have a deal."

During the years that he pastored, my brother, Dr. Robert Cornwall, was never called to a large church and never left a small one behind. God has graced him with the ability to build churches into several thousand members. In his last pastorate in Oregon, he had over ninety people on his church staff, and nearly three thousand members in his congregation.

He told me, "One of the pressures of seeking to minister to a large congregation is handling the responsibility of meeting the needs of the various departments of that congregation. All of them cry for help, but there are not enough hours in the day to meet all the needs."

"Now that I am in a traveling ministry," Robert continued, "I find that many pastors are frustrated simply because they have not taken the time to figure out what they are responsible to do and what responsibilities must be delegated to other staff members."

"Delegating responsibility is essential," I interrupted.

"Essential? Yes. Easy? No!" Robert responded. "Whenever I considered bringing another person on staff, I handed the candidate a portfolio with a complete job description. If we employed a person, I took time to go over that job description with them very carefully. I wanted each person on my staff to understand his or her role in our total church program. I impressed upon the staff workers that the associate pastor's job was not the music, and the music minister's role was not the Sunday school. The church would be ministered to properly when each department head functioned within the parameters of his or her job description."

Robert observed, and I can confirm, that many modern pastors are collapsing emotionally because of overwork. They try to do everything the members of the congregation expect of them instead of determining the boundaries for their personal and active involvement. Each pastor must decide what he sees as his or her major job and what is but a minor part of the ministry. Anything the pastor does not accept as his responsibility must be delegated to someone else. All ministry must be attended to, but not everything need be done by one person.

"Does this have anything to do with spiritual warfare?" you might ask. It does! One reason we are so out of balance in our spiritual warfare is that we have ignored scriptural job descriptions and exhausted ourselves in unassigned activities. We depart from our assigned role and try to pick up a role that God has assigned to someone else.

God, Who is an efficient manager, has clearly defined the role of each of the four active participants in the scheme of redemption—Jesus, the Holy Spirit, the Church, and the angels. When each follows the guidelines of the job description given by God, the work progresses smoothly and effectively. When one forsakes the assigned role, however, and seeks to function in the role given to another, two roles go unfulfilled. Worst of all, we frustrate the purpose of the cross of Jesus.

The Role for Jesus

Paul clearly states that God the Father and Jesus, His Son, work together in the program of redemption. He wrote: *"All things are of God, who hath reconciled us to himself by Jesus Christ, and hath given to us the ministry of reconciliation; To wit, that God was in Christ, reconciling the world unto himself, not imputing their trespasses unto them; and hath committed unto us the word of reconciliation."*

The job description the Father gave to Jesus is redemption of the lost and their reconciliation to fellowship with God. As I have described in my book, *The Sprinkled Blood,* this required Christ to become our substitute. There is a final statement in Paul's report:

> *For he [God] hath made him [Jesus] to be sin for us, who knew no sin; that we might be made the righteousness of God in him.* 2 Corinthians 5:21

All Christ's work on the cross was vicarious—that is, serving in the place of someone else. We could not redeem ourselves, because *"The wages of sin is death; but the gift of God is eternal life through Jesus Christ our Lord"* (Romans 6:23). Only Jesus could take our place, pay our penalty, and rise from the dead to remain as our Intercessor at the right hand of the Father. His was an exclusive role that none other could fill.

We cannot redeem ourselves. The Holy Spirit did not become a man, so He could never take our place, and angels cannot die, so they could not pay the penalty we deserved. The job description the Father gave to Jesus applied to Him alone.

While Jesus was fulfilling His mission of redemption, He healed the sick, performed miracles, and taught like a prophet. If He had chosen to major in those fields, He could have become a world-renowned prophet or a popular worker of miracles. This is exactly what the people of His day wanted Him to do. They even wanted to make Him king. Although Jesus was both capable and willing to fill these roles, however, He constantly reminded Himself that God had assigned these roles to others. He dared not major in minors. He had a more serious job to do, and if He failed, God had no backup redeemer.

Keeping the ministry of the cross before Him had to be a daily decision for Jesus. Mary, Martha, and Lazarus offered home comforts that were pleasant to the Master, and there must have been times He would have wanted to trade itinerant ministry for the serenity of a peaceful home in Bethany. Bethany, however, would not provide a cross.

Human nature being what it is, it is very possible that Mary Magdalene was attractive to Jesus. She was devoted to Him and unashamedly poured out her love on Him. Jesus may have considered the pleasures and security of marriage, but God did not commission Jesus to marry and raise a family. He came as the Savior of the world, and He never veered from that calling—regardless of what else may have seemed attractive to Him along the way.

Any number of natural desires must have entered the mind of Jesus, and these were not evil thoughts. They simply would have prevented Him from executing the perfect will of God.

People almost certainly would have nudged Jesus consistently to find fulfillment in a more standard form of life, but He would not be deterred from His mission. When He told His disciples that He would suffer many things of the elders, chief priest and scribes in Jerusalem and then be killed and raised from the dead on the third day, their reaction was violent:

> *Then Peter took him, and began to rebuke him, saying, Be it far from thee, LORD: this shall not be unto thee. But he turned, and said unto Peter, Get thee behind me, Satan: thou art an offence unto me: for*

thou savourest not the things that be of God, but those that be of men. Matthew 16:22-23

Even His handpicked and personally-trained disciples sought to turn Jesus from His job designation. He had to rebuke Peter, for He heard the sound of Satan's voice in what Peter said.

In his gospel narrative, Dr. Luke said of Jesus:

It came to pass, when the time was come that he should be received up, he stedfastly set his face to go to Jerusalem, And sent messengers before his face: and they went, and entered into a village of the Samaritans, to make ready for him. And they did not receive him, because his face was as though he would go to Jerusalem. Luke 9:51-53

Everyone had a personal agenda for Jesus. When He ignored the desires of men and set Himself determinately to fulfill the agenda His Father had set for Him, people rejected Him. He accepted that rejection as part of doing the will of God. No other need could be allowed to supersede God's will. He had come to redeem men from sin and unto a reconciled standing with God, and nothing could deter Him from that course.

The Role of the Holy Spirit

Like the pastor of a growing church, Jesus realized that although He could faithfully fulfil His role, He could not do the entire job by Himself. He needed a support team—workers who would capably do what He could not do without impeding His redemptive work. God the Father commissioned the Holy Spirit to be a co-laborer with Jesus in reconciling the world to God.

The Holy Spirit was not a direct participant in redemption. That was the specific work of Jesus. The role the Father gave to the Spirit is of Convictor or Convincer. Jesus said of the Spirit:

> *Nevertheless I tell you the truth; It is expedient for you that I go away: for if I go not away, the Comforter will not come unto you, but if I depart, I will send him unto you. And when he is come, he will reprove the world of sin, and of righteousness, and of judgment: Of sin, because they believe not on me; Of righteousness, because I go to my Father, and ye see me no more; Of judgment, because the prince of this world is judged.* John 16:7-11

The Greek word we translate here "reprove" is *elegeho*, which means "to tell a fault, convict, convince, rebuke, or reprove." He, Who is a special Comforter to the Church, functions as a prosecuting attorney to the world. His special commission is to:

1. Reprove the world of sin, because men and women do not believe on Jesus and His finished work
2. Convict of righteousness, because Jesus went to the Father and was no longer a visible demonstration of the righteousness of God
3. Convince men and women of judgment, because the prince of this world was judged and

proclaimed guilty at Calvary and his authority is nonexistent

The Holy Spirit flowed into this office in a most demonstrative way. On the Day of Pentecost He came as a mighty rushing wind and a cloven tongue of fire (see Acts 2). The effects in Jerusalem were startling. While He brought confirming signs of Christ's acceptance in Heaven that produced peace in the hearts of the men and women in the Upper Room, His same presence brought mass conviction in Jerusalem. People who had never felt conviction crumbled under its weight.

Those who laughed at the disciples in the garden, the paid false accusers, the soldier who had won the raffle for Christ's robe, and those in the multitude who had scoffed at Jesus on His way to Golgotha now felt the fear of stark conviction as it struck their hearts through the presence of the Holy Spirit.

"My God, I'm wrong!" was their cry. This city-wide conviction of wrongdoing that the Holy Spirit produced on that Day of Pentecost explains the three thousand conversions that occurred after Peter's anointed sermon and the five thousand conversions that occurred a few days later.

Throughout the book of Acts, we see the Holy Spirit working as a prosecutor, convincing men and women of their rejection of Christ, their unholy lives, and their ignorance of Satan's powerless condition. Paul was a channel for this convicting work of the Spirit everywhere he went. He turned entire cities upside down, often in just a few days.

Just as in Genesis 1:2, *"The Spirit of God moved upon*

the face of the waters," preparing the Earth for the intervention of God that would transform it from a void to a viable world, so the Holy Spirit moves as a brooding force upon the hearts of men and women, preparing them to hear the Gospel of redemption and be saved. The Holy Spirit convicts, to the point of terror, those who have not accepted Jesus Christ as their Lord and Savior. There can be no effective evangelization without this convicting work of the Spirit. While Christ has paid the price for the conversion of every man, woman, boy, or girl in the world, this redemption is not effective until it is embraced personally. The Holy Spirit's special role is to incite, pressure, and goad men and women into accepting God's free provision in Christ Jesus.

No matter how hard we may try with our witnessing or preaching, we cannot produce this conviction. This is the job description of the third person of the Trinity. Education has never replaced the conviction of the Holy Spirit. Emotion cannot produce true conviction. The facts of education and the feeling of emotion are weak substitutes for the dynamic convicting power of the Holy Spirit.

The Scriptures declare that the Holy Spirit is at work, drawing men to Christ. Some men He drives, some He leads, and others He nudges. Whatever the means employed, this is His special portfolio. He is limited, however. He cannot preach the Gospel. He can only convict and reveal what will happen to men if they do not repent when they hear it.

This special work of the Spirit to the world differs greatly from His work in the Church. In the Church,

He comforts, encourages, and empowers the members of Christ's universal Body. He acts as the prompter in a play, bringing back to our memories things Jesus has taught us. He, by Christ's orders, brings us into all truth.

The Role of the Church

The Father assigned the job description of reconciliation to Jesus. He appointed the Holy Spirit to the ministry of conviction, but He specifically commissioned His Church to the ministry of proclamation. We are to preach, teach, and be a witness to the Gospel, the good news of redemption through Christ.

Try as we will, the Church cannot redeem men and women or reconcile them to God. Only Jesus can do that. The Church universal cannot convict men and women of sin, righteousness, and judgment. We can merely talk about it. Christ's Great Commission to His disciples, and to us, is:

> *Go ye therefore, and teach all nations, baptizing them in the name of the Father, and of the Son, and of the Holy Ghost: Teaching them to observe all things whatsoever I have commanded you: and, lo, I am with you alway, even unto the end of the world. Amen.* Matthew 28:19-20

We, the Church, are given the job description of teaching, baptizing, and demonstrating the presence of Christ in us. We are not producers; we are proclaimers. We are not the agents of redemption; we are merely the announcers of redemption.

Whose Role Is It, Anyway?

We live in a sin-infested society where people are guilt-ridden and hopeless, but we have good news to proclaim to this world. God has commissioned us to divulge a secret. It is:

> *There is one God, and one mediator between God and men, the man Christ Jesus.* 1 Timothy 2:5

We are called to a ministry of reconciliation:

> *[God] hath reconciled us to himself by Jesus Christ, and hath given to us the ministry of reconciliation.*
> 2 Corinthians 5:18

Our ministry of reconciliation is not to try to replace the Reconciliator, but to reveal the reconciliation. God has disclosed the redemptive plan to us, and He has challenged us to declare that revelation to men and women who are still locked in darkness.

We cannot do the work of reconciliation, but the Reconciliator, now in Heaven, also cannot broadcast the good news that the work has been done without our help. God has given us that privilege. We are *"workers together with him"* (2 Corinthians 6:1).

We are not the convincer; that is the job of the Holy Spirit. If we become negative in our proclamations, trying to preach sin instead of preaching Christ, we abandon our assigned roles and step into the role of the Holy Spirit. Christ did not appoint us to preach about sin; our job description is to preach about the Savior. The Good News is not conviction, but release from conviction. We proclaim that repentance (the

Greek word we translate "repent" means a one-hundred-and-eighty-degree turn) will release men and women from conviction and enable them to embrace a Great Redeemer.

When the people of Lystra reacted to the demonstration of the power of God through Paul and Barnabas by pronouncing them gods and preparing to offer sacrifices to them, Paul declared:

> *We also are men of like passions with you, and preach unto you that ye should turn from these vanities unto the living God, which made heaven, and earth, and the sea, and all things that are therein.*
>
> Acts 14:15

Paul rejected the role of divinity. He refused to replace Jesus or the Holy Spirit. Although he had the presence of Jesus in his life and the power of the Holy Spirit in his ministry, he insisted on remaining in his assigned role as a proclaimer, and so should we.

Paul's message was not the sin of Lystra but that they should *"turn unto the living God,"* and that is our message as well. Men already know they are sinners. They live with a sublimated guilt in their consciences that rises to dominate their thinking when in the presence of the Holy Spirit. They don't need this defined as much as they need to know how to get rid of it. That is the Good News we have been sent to proclaim.

Our assignment is quite simple: tell the world to turn around. My brother Robert often speaks of "cat sense." He has observed that if you stroke a cat from its tail to its head, it will turn around to make the stroking com-

comfortable. He likens that to conversion. The ministry of the Church is to teach people "cat sense." Our message to men and women is for them to turn around so that the miserable stroke of conviction will become a comforting stroke of love and acceptance. It occurs automatically when men and women turn from their willful ways to the ways of God.

"Turn" was the message of the Old Testament prophets. *"Turn from your wicked ways"* and *"turn unto the Lord your God."* This was also the message of the apostles, and it must again become the message of the Church.

Why has the church departed from *"the simplicity that is in Christ"* (2 Corinthians 11:3)? We are like the associate pastor who wants to take on the job of senior pastor or like the Christian education director who wants to lead the choir. We may interact with Christ and the Holy Spirit, but we have a job that they cannot do without us—any more than we can do it without them. It may seem that our job is too simple, but it is always commensurate with our capabilities.

When we stay within our job descriptions, we need not worry about pulling down the "strongholds" of Satan. We have been sent to rescue those whom Satan has taken captive. We have been commissioned to inform them that God has arranged a full pardon for them. The prison doors have been opened, and the prisoner is authorized to return to a life of freedom in Christ Jesus.

Incarcerated people don't need a sermon about their jailor. They know every guard by name and nature. What they want and need to hear is, "You are pardoned. Jesus has finished your sentence for you."

Bearers of the good news of a pardon do not need to storm the penitentiary. The warden does not need to be bound, nor do the guards need to be put in cells. The authority for release comes from the highest source. There is no position of authority in the prison that can countermand a pardon. Why, then, try to launch a frontal attack on Satan's prison? If we will stay with our job description, we can release men from the bondage of Satan into the perfect liberty of sonship in God.

The Role of the Angels

The staff that God has assembled to minister to the needs of the world He loves is not complete with the presence of Jesus, the Holy Spirit and the Church. He has also appointed His angels to be part of this ministry team.

The Father has assigned the Church to function in a world that is cruel, malicious, and antagonistic to the Gospel. Like prisoners who are anti-establishment, the world automatically hates God. Out of that response to the conviction of the Holy Spirit comes an angry response to those who have been channels for the work of the Spirit. Jesus said:

> *If the world hate you, ye know that it hated me before it hated you. If ye were of the world, the world would love his own: but because ye are not of the world, but I have chosen you out of the world, therefore the world hateth you.* John 15:18-19

We have a glorious message of good news, but we

are feared, despised, and persecuted because our lives are so different. Jesus prophesied this when He said:

> *Behold, I send you forth as sheep in the midst of wolves: be ye therefore wise as serpents, and harmless as doves.* Matthew 10:16

> *Go your ways: behold, I send you forth as lambs among wolves.* Luke 10:3

What defense have sheep against wolves? No lamb can survive an attack from a wolf. So, has God cruelly set up His Church for early martyrdom? No! A thousand times no! He has provided for His Church to live, not die.

Why, then, did Jesus tell His disciples to put aside their swords, and to turn the other cheek to those who struck them? It seems that not only are we inherently defenseless, we are prohibited from learning defensive tactics or from carrying weapons for our own protection.

Jesus knew that there was an enemy just waiting for a chance to attack the Church in general and individual members of the Body of Christ in particular, yet He has provided us with only defensive armor. We have no attack weapons. Why? Because defense is not the assignment given to the Church. This is the role God gave to His angels.

Throughout the New Testament, whenever members of the Church were doing what the Church was called to do, God's angels became their protectors. Peter, for instance, was imprisoned and scheduled to be executed. The night before he was to die, however, an angel of the Lord came into his cell, awakened him, caused his shackles to fall off his hands and feet and led him out of the prison. Closed doors and gates opened as they went. Neither Peter nor the other disciples could withstand the might of Rome, but God's angels became their defense.

When the president of the United States leaves the White House, he knows he walks in potential danger. Still, he never carries a gun. He relies on the Secret Service agents who accompany him to be his security. He does his job as the head of State, and they do their job of warding off any threats of harm to the Commander-in-Chief.

When we are out on a mission spreading the Good News, God's secret agents—His angels—surround us. They are our defense against both men and demons. They can defuse the anger in the hearts of men.

At the conclusion of a session in a minister's conference, my wife and another pastor's wife rushed to the platform saying, "Did you see them?"

"See who," I asked.

"The angels," they excitedly responded. "They went through the audience with thermometers taking the temperature of the ministers. When they found one with a high temperature of anger, they put hands on his head and calmed him."

I had been unaware that my message was creating such anger, but the angels knew it and took prompt action against it. Angels are our defenders, even though they are not under our command. They are the angels of the Lord, and He is their Commander.

Paul asked, *"Know ye not that we shall judge angels?"* (1 Corinthians 6:3). This is clearly for a future day, for most of us barely have an idea of what angels do.

Let us stick to what we do well and leave the realm of protection to God's Secret Service. Trust God's mighty army of angels to war against demonic forces while we loudly proclaim the Gospel of grace to fallen men and women.

Whenever angels are needed, they are present. It was true in the lives of Moses, Joshua, David, Peter, Paul, and Jesus. Even when God delivered Jesus into the hands of Satan at Calvary, angels were there to protect Him. They insisted that nothing more be done to Christ than the Father had agreed upon. They saw to it that Jesus died before the other two crucified victims. They also prevented the soldiers from breaking His legs. They were there to safeguard every facet of Christ's death so it would completely fulfill the Scriptures.

All this was beyond the control of Jesus. He had given Himself into the hands of His tormentors and had made Himself helpless in their hands. Nothing of what happened that day was beyond the control of Father God, however. He worked through His mighty angels to see that His will was accomplished.

Angels are for our spiritual protection, so we need not try to protect ourselves. Angels are able to do a far better job of this than we could, and they have been given the portfolio of protecting the saints.

When the Church stops worrying about its protection and again gets involved in turning men around to face the grace of God, it will release the angels to do their task of protecting us. It is not that we are totally without defensive weapons. We can rebuke the devil, and he will flee from us. We can apply the blood covenant against the enemy, and he will back off, but we must not go beyond our job description.

When we get busy trying to defeat the devil, he wins because he has sidetracked us from our designated job—sharing the Good News with others. While we are doing the job of angels, they are unable to do our job of preaching and witnessing.

Stop striving. Paul told his spiritual son Timothy:

> *The servant of the* LORD *must not strive; but be gentle unto all men, apt to teach, patient, In meekness instructing those that oppose themselves; if God peradventure will give them repentance to the acknowledging of the truth; And that they may recover themselves out of the snare of the devil, who are taken captive by him at his will.* 2 Timothy 2:24

We must recognize that Satan is already a defeated foe. Our role is to yield ourselves to God and to teach the Good News that will enable people to recover themselves out of the snare of the devil. We need not worry about destroying the devil; God will do that in His time. In the meantime, we must go about opening the traps that have our friends ensnared.

Jesus has done his job of redemption and reconciliation, the Holy Spirit continues to fulfill His mission to convict men of sin, and the angels always stand at attention to protect the spreading of the Good News. Now God is waiting for the Church to do its assigned task.

Let us get our eyes off Satan and focus them on God.

Let us stop trying to do the Spirit's work of conviction and allow Him to work through us. Most importantly, let us stop pretending that we are angels and function as the human beings God made us to be.

We cannot preach the finished work of Calvary if we are out trying to finish it for Christ. We cannot proclaim Good News if we are involved in the bad news of struggling with the devil. Let us do what God has called us to do. Preach victory over Satan; don't try to produce it.

God has not erred in assigning the tasks. Trust Him that He knows exactly what He is doing, and then let Him do things His way.

CHAPTER 7

WHOSE STRATEGY IS IT, ANYWAY?

Now the Spirit speaketh expressly, that in the latter times some shall depart from the faith, giving heed to seducing spirits, and doctrines of devils.

1 Timothy 4:1

I was invited by a group of ministers to a meeting where an attempt would be made to map out a strategy for defeating Satan in the United States. Ministers from many different denominations and groups would be in attendance. Although I highly respected many of those who would be part of this conference, I declined the invitation. It seemed to me that it was too late to contemplate such a lofty goal. Christ had already defeated Satan, and I saw no need to reinvent Calvary. If Christ's strategy had not worked, what chance had we mere mortals of coming up with a plan that would succeed?

Since I did not attend that particular meeting, I can say nothing about what was shared there. I do know, however, some of the themes being taught in these circles, and I can say that I simply cannot agree with many of them.

In my way of thinking, one of the most serious errors being perpetuated is the teaching concerning generational or hereditary demon control of one's life.

The feeling is that demon possession (some more gently call it "demon oppression") can be transmitted genetically. Those who espouse this doctrine teach that if one can discover the point of entrance of the demonic force into his or her family line, victory over it can be achieved. The strategy used is to help the person reconstruct his or her family tree as far back as possible—all the while seeking evidence of demonic activity in that heritage.

The Apostle Paul did not seem to understand this form of ministry, for he taught:

> *Therefore if any man be in Christ, he is a new creature: old things are passed away; behold, all things are become new.* 2 Corinthians 5:17

The New International Version of the Bible translates this verse as: *"He is a new creation; the old has gone, the new has come!"* If, when a person comes to Christ, his old life passes away and a totally new life comes into being, what value is there to digging in the graveyard of that old life?

It is my observation that most of what these persons dig up in the generational search and attribute to the work of demons are the same things Paul referred to as *"the works of the flesh."* In the same passage that deals with the fruit of the Spirit, Paul wrote:

> *Now the works of the flesh are manifest, which are these; Adultery, fornication, uncleanness, lasciviousness, Idolatry, witchcraft, hatred, variance, emulations, wrath, strife, seditions, heresies,*

Envyings, murders, drunkenness, revellings, and such like: of the which I tell you before, as I have also told you in time past, that they which do such things shall not inherit the kingdom of God.
Galatians 5:19-21

There may be predispositions to these works that are hereditary or generational, but that doesn't make it a result of demonic activity. Paul showed that these deportments express the innate nature of men under sin. This should be dealt with at the cross, not in deliverance ministry.

Some who embrace this idea of hereditary demonic possession try everything short of hypnosis to cause the patient to recall things beyond his or her conscious memory. Some even presume to cause a person to remember experiences they had while still in the womb. If highly trained professional psychologists and psychiatrists are unable to produce cures for people with the traits Paul mentioned using these same methods, what makes us think that totally untrained, however enthusiastic, laymen can bring people to deliverance using them? These people are playing with very dangerous tools, and those guilty of doing it may do far more damage than good—if they persist.

Salvation cannot be transmitted genetically. The Word of God makes it perfectly clear that none can be born saved. I found it necessary to tell each of my three daughters that my salvation would not automatically become theirs just because I was a preacher of the Gospel. They had to open their lives by an act of their wills and receive Jesus as their own personal Savior.

Why would we believe that Satan has more power than Jesus? If Christ cannot be transmitted genetically, what is the basis of our belief that Satan or demons can be passed on from one generation to another? Predisposition may be transmitted, but more likely it is the case that the home environment gives greater opportunity to accept Christ or to open oneself to demonic activity. This is not inheritance; it is mere association.

Many of us do not sufficiently appreciate our Christian heritage. What a blessing it is to have been born into a truly Christian home! Early familiarity with the Bible, prayer, and a community of believers in a church setting have opened us to the ways of God far more than we may have realized.

The converse is also true. Those who were reared in homes of wickedness or, worse yet, in homes that practiced demonology openly, are more easily sensitized to demonic activity in their lives. The fact that a person has been raised in darkness, however, does not mean that he or she need remain there. Jesus said:

> *I am the light of the world: he that followeth me shall not walk in darkness, but shall have the light of life.* John 8:12

People with a heritage of darkness need not examine that darkness, nor is it important that they know at what point they entered that darkness. They need light, and when Christ comes in, He is that light. These persons need teaching and training, not witch hunting into their past and the past of their family members.

While I have no way of knowing what percentage

of believers currently embrace the idea of generational demonic possession, I see at work throughout much of the Christian world a three-pronged strategy against the devil. It might be summed up as: reduction, relocation and restriction of the devil.

The Reduction Strategy

The *reduction strategy* presumes to pull down the strongholds of the devil. The idea is that Satan has appointed key personnel over every country and over every city. Many even believe that specific demons have been assigned to each local congregation and its destruction.

The only scriptural basis being offered for this belief is the passage in the book of Daniel where the angel, who was sent with an answer to Daniel's prayer, apologized for the delay in getting the answer back by saying:

> *The prince of the kingdom of Persia withstood me one and twenty days: but, lo, Michael, one of the chief princes, came to help me; and I remained there with the kings of Persia.* Daniel 10:13

This verse has become a rallying cry for saints to assemble and do warfare with the prince over a geographic district. The gathered faithful are told to *"pull down the strongholds."* Often the leaders give believers the name of the prince who holds control over that area. Sometimes the name of this prince is given in a prophetic manner, and other times his name is deduced from the name of the city or its basic culture.

Once they feel that they know the name of the satanic entity who has control of that area, these people feel authorized to call him by name and command him to come down. They seek to reduce him from the heavens above us to the Earth beneath us. This is folly. Although you might be angry with the president of your local bank, you have no authority to fire him and replace him with another. Since we did not place spirit forces in power in the atmosphere above us, we lack the power to take them out of power or to reduce their office from activity in the heavens above to action on the Earth beneath. Nothing we can do will change that fact.

If it took Michael (whom God earlier commissioned to cast Satan out of Heaven) to release the angel sent to Daniel, what makes us think that poor redeemed mortals like us can give orders that will be obeyed by princes over geographic regions?

Basing belief and behavior upon this one reference in Scripture is dangerous, for the Scriptures warn:

> *In the mouth of two or three witnesses every word may be established.* Matthew 18:16

> *This is the third time I am coming to you. In the mouth of two or three witnesses shall every word be established.* 2 Corinthians 13:1

The passage in Daniel relates a conflict between an angel from Heaven and a high-level demonic power that governed Persia. While it does illustrate that human government may be demonically influenced and even controlled, it does not teach that this is so of all governments or that Satan has high-level forces over each nation or each city, and certainly not over each local church.

We would not dare to deduce that because Balaam's ass spoke to him, all well-bred asses have the power of human speech. We would not dare to say that because Jesus walked on water, all of us should be doing it on a daily basis. It is dangerous to project too much from a single incident in Scripture.

Although the passage from Daniel gives us a faint view into the dark spirit world, we cannot build a doctrine on this one glimpse. God has shared with us very little knowledge about Satan's kingdom. What we do know about him is that he sends forth *"seducing spirits"* that produce *"doctrines of devils":*

When we become involved in activities that exalt Satan and his works, we are falling into the trap of his *"seducing spirits."* Satan would love nothing more than to exhaust the church by tricking us into fighting a mirage.

The Relocation Strategy

Not everyone in the spiritual warfare camp has chosen to get involved with pulling down high-level spiritual forces. Some are content to demand the *relocation* of spirit beings. Their specialty is casting Satan out and consigning him to the pit. While they generally use the term "Satan," they are actually dealing with demon spirits.

I was present when a leader explained that through revelation, he had learned that spirits hate uninhabited, dry places. Accordingly, he sends expelled demons "to the desert places." Since I live in Phoenix, a desert area, I instinctively resent this. We don't need any more demons in Arizona. While Jesus did give us authority to free men and women from demonic activity, He did not give us the authority to tell them exactly where to go.

When men say that they are assigning a demon "to the pit," what do they mean by that? Are they referring to *"the bottomless pit"* mentioned in Revelation 9:1-2? God has locked it, and only an angel of God can unlock it. How, then, can we get a demon into the place?

We often defeat our purposes with improper religious jargon, and I suspect that Satan has distorted some of our religious terminology in an attempt to prevent us from flowing into real truth.

I write my books on a computer using WordPerfect 7.0 as my word processor. I have hundreds of commands at my finger tips. When I type those commands correctly, they are obeyed almost instantly. When, however, I add something to my command that is not in the program, I draw a complete blank—or worse. Sometimes I even wipe out some of my material by inadvertently entering a wrong command. A computer is a very useful tool, but it will do only what the program has instructed it to do and only when I give it correct and specific commands. As long as we overstate our spiritual authority, there can be no compliance with our true authority.

The Restriction Strategy

Another prong of the tactics used by many of those engaged in spiritual warfare is the *restriction* of the devil. They are forever binding him. There is nothing wrong with their motivation in doing this. They would like to incapacitate the devil and demons so they can never again cause pain, blindness, or bondage in the lives of Christians. Correct motivations, however, do not always produce correct movements. Is binding the devil within the jurisdiction of the Church? The jurisdictional authority for this action comes from the words of Jesus, Who said:

> *I will give unto thee the keys of the kingdom of heaven: and whatsoever thou shalt bind on earth shall be bound in heaven: and whatsoever thou shalt loose on earth shall be loosed in heaven.*
>
> Matthew 16:19

> *Whatsoever ye shall bind on earth shall be bound in heaven: and whatsoever ye shall loose on earth shall be loosed in heaven.* Matthew 18:18

The first time Jesus uttered this phrase (Matthew 16:19) was immediately following Peter's declaration that Jesus was the Christ. Satan and his kingdom are not in the context. This passage is concerned with Christ and His Kingdom. The second time Jesus spoke of binding and loosing on Earth (Matthew 18:18) was in the context of seeking reconciliation with a brother or sister in the church. There is nothing in this context that speaks of the devil.

Perhaps those who bind the devil are correct in extrapolating this passage to include the satanic realm. Personally, I do not feel that this is sound interpretation of what Jesus said, but I am not the total authority on the teachings of Jesus. If persons of faith can actually bind demons, however, why are they still around and so active? Why not just bind them all and do away with their activity once and for all? Satan is still subtle and has, I fear, confused many of us on this issue.

The strategies of men have never worked against the powers of the devil. It is about time we return to God's Book, the Bible, and see what His strategies are for His Church.

The Captain's Strategies in the Old Testament

As we saw in Chapter 3, the Captain of the hosts of the Lord became Israel's strategist in the conquest of the Promised Land. Although Joshua was always the visible leader, this Captain, who was actually Jesus, gave all the battle orders. The tactics He put forth were so successful that Israel defeated the armies of the seven nations that dwelt in the Promised Land without losing a single Hebrew soldier—except in the rebellious incident of Ai.

Many methods commonly used in spiritual warfare are adaptations from the conquest of the Promise Land under the leadership of Joshua and God's Captain. Leaders project that what God did then, He will continue to do now. Fundamentally that is correct, but the weakness in the premise is the assumption that God always does things the same way. This very book they quote proves that God is infinitely varied. He never used the same method of warfare against two cities. Every action was different.

The Captain's method for capturing Jericho was to have the Israelites march around the wall in silence every day for seven days, and on the seventh day they marched around Jericho seven times. At a God-given signal, they shouted, and the walls fell down. This doesn't mean that every Jericho march will have the same success.

In fighting the coalition army of five nations, God chose to use giant hailstones to kill the enemy armies. Since warfare in the time of Joshua was hand-to-hand fighting, these killer hailstones had to be aimed very carefully. It was more than a thunderstorm. Angels were throwing hailstones like baseballs, and their accuracy was amazing, for these killer hailstones did not hit even one Israelite soldier. This method of fighting was never again used in the conquest of Canaan. Each battle was unique, and this called for fresh faith in God's leadership.

This principle proved to be true with David's conquest of the lands surrounding Israel after he came to the throne. As skillful a warrior as he was, David consistently looked to the Lord for direction in his battle plans. He never dared used any method just because it had worked before. Sometimes, following a frontal attack, God would have him lay in ambush and send a small division of soldiers to attack the city and then fall back. When the defenders opened the gates to pursue the retreating foe, the concealed army rose up, entered and destroyed the city.

God's tactics, when Gideon was God's front man, included the use of torches, pitchers, and trumpets. God instructed Gideon to take a position on the hills overlooking the enemy encampment. He was to leave the valley gap between the mountains open for the enemy's retreat. When the pitchers were broken, revealing the torches of Gideon's valiant three hundred men, and when they had blown their trumpets, terror gripped the hearts of the Midianites, and they fled through the narrow gap Gideon had left open.

By leaving the enemy a place to retreat, God averted the necessity of a direct confrontation. In the darkness and confusion, the Midianites slew one another as they fled. Self-destruction has consistently been a favorite tool of God. Gideon's army merely conducted a mopping-up maneuver. As daring and successful as the methods Gideon employed were, God never again used them in exactly the same way. He is so creative and original that He need not repeat Himself in anything.

Throughout the Old Testament, we see God using different tactics in leading His people against their enemies. When the kings of Israel, Judah, and Edom joined forces to defeat the Moabites, God instructed them, through Elisha the prophet, to dig ditches in the valley. During the night, God filled those ditches with water, and when the morning sun reflected off the water, the Moabites saw it as blood and assumed that the three kings had turned upon each other in a great slaughter. Hastily they rushed into the valley to take the spoils, and the three kings soundly defeated them. This tactic, too, was never repeated in the written records.

When we walk and work *with* the Lord, there will

be infinite variety. On the other hand, when we just religiously work *for* the Lord, we often establish ritual that we repeat endlessly. Working *with* the Lord requires a living, active faith, but working *for* the Lord in repeated ritual takes little more than an average memory.

If God's Methods are Varied, Why are Ours Predictable?

Copying the way God did things in the past seldom wins victories in the present. We are frequently reminded of the great victory God gave to Jehoshaphat, king of Judah. A great coalition army came against him, causing him to cry out to the Lord. God's answer was:

> *Ye shall not need to fight in this battle: set yourselves, stand ye still, and see the salvation of the LORD with you, O Judah and Jerusalem: fear not, nor be dismayed; to-morrow go out against them: for the LORD will be with you.*
>
> 2 Chronicles 20:17

The next day, when the Israelites went out to meet the enemy, Jehoshaphat sent the musicians in the front of the army to sing and praise the Lord. When the armies of Israel arrived at the enemy encampment, they found that their tormentors were already dead—most of them slain in an internal conflict that turned them one against another.

These musicians went forth to praise and magnify God Who had slain the enemy. They were rejoicing, by faith, in a finished work, and so should we. The only thing required of Jehoshaphat's army was that it spend three days gathering up the spoils of battle.

Worshiping saints rejoice when faced by an enemy because they know that it's God's war, and He will destroy their enemy.

God's Principles Remain Constant

There are principles that remain constant. One is that God usually leaves a retreat path for the enemy. God always preferred to have His people chase an enemy rather than confront him head on. A second principle in God's warfare is that He is the leader. He gives the orders; we obey them. God wants our faith and obedience far more than He wants our cleverness and daring. If, indeed, it's God's war, then we would do well to let Him order every battle and try not to interfere with His plan.

Not once in the record of Israel's conquests do we see them in a contest with spiritual powers over cities or countries. If any such contest occurred, God assigned the angels to the task and kept His people focused on their true enemies. We have enough struggle with the enemy in our minds without trying to replace the angels in contending with high-level satanic powers.

Some of the emphasis given in many spiritual warfare conferences is dangerous for the emotional balance of those participating. Some Christians come away from these meeting seeing demons under every rock and behind every tree. They feel that it is necessary to rebuke the devil at every turn of the road, and to "plead the blood" before driving to the corner store. This is incompatible with the warfare God led in the Old Testament, and it is certainly inconsistent with Christ's war strategy in the New.

CHRIST'S STRATEGIES IN THE NEW TESTAMENT

When we get to the New Testament, the concept of battle turns from human enemies to spiritual forces. Jesus Christ came to combat the forces of Satan and sin and gloriously defeated them at Calvary. As the Captain of our salvation, He continues to lead us into spiritual victories we could never obtain by ourselves. He has a three-pronged strategy. One prong is against the devil, a second is on behalf of the Church on Earth, and a third concerns individual Christians in their day-to-day conflict with unrighteousness.

Christ's strategy in His conquest of Satan was to strip him. We looked at this in Chapter 2 and saw that Christ removed from Satan every title, symbol of authority, and vestige of power. This happened during Christ's ascension. He made an open display of this conquest of Satan to every satanic power on Earth before taking these visible symbols to Heaven where they are now on display in Heaven's trophy room.

During Christ's ministry, and through His work on the cross, Jesus systematically destroyed the works of the devil. John tells us:

> *For this purpose the Son of God was manifested, that he might destroy the works of the devil.*
>
> 1 John 3:8

The Greek word that is translated as "destroy" in this verse is *luo,* a word used only twice in the New Testament. Strong's concordance says *luo* means "to loosen—break up—dissolve—unloose—melt—put off—or put loose." The root from which this word comes means "to wreck; to sunder (by separation of the parts)."

There is a great mystery about the devil and God's progressive dealing with him. Paul wrote:

> *And now ye know what withholdeth that he may be revealed in his time. For the mystery of iniquity doth already work: only he who now letteth will let, until he be taken out of the way. And then shall that Wicked be revealed, whom the Lord shall consume with the spirit of his mouth, and shall destroy with the brightness of his coming.*
>
> 2 Thessalonians 2:6-8

Although Satan has been dispossessed from Heaven and was dethroned at Christ's crucifixion and subsequent ascension, Jesus did not come to destroy the devil. Satan will never be destroyed. Eventually God will permanently consign him in the Lake of Fire, but he will live endlessly. Jesus came to destroy *"the works of the devil."* As evangelist Dr. Fuchsia Pickett likes to say, "Jesus came to undo, redo, and overdo the works of the devil."

John's choice of the Greek word *luo* to describe Christ's present method of destroying the works of the devil is exceptional in its descriptive power. Presently Jesus does not prevent Satan from working. His works, as the prince of darkness, supreme liar, arch-sinner and master rebel, have actually accelerated since his expulsion from Heaven. His deceitful and murderous nature still works among men and women.

Christ's coming into the world and His death at Calvary undid everything that Satan has done or ever will do. Christ causes it to dissolve, melt, or be torn asunder. It is as though God forces Satan to use untempered mortar in anything he builds, and the bricks fall apart. Jesus allows him to show his fine craftsmanship in constructing a coffee table, but his glue is rotten, and the table falls apart the first time something is placed on it. It is as though Satan is allowed to design fine clothes, but as he sews them, his bobbin is always out of thread. When he holds the garment up for inspection, it falls apart onto the floor.

Satan is not prevented from working. Jesus merely causes everything he does to break up, melt, or be dismantled. How frustrating this must be! It hardly seems worthwhile for saints to contend so earnestly against such a loser. The presence of Jesus will break up the works of Satan, whether those works be pride, rebellion, misdirected worship, or self-will. The purpose of our worship is to touch the presence of God, and that presence becomes the death knell for the works of the devil.

We Are the Sheep of His Pasture

Christ's strategy for His Church is to lead it like a Shepherd. We are the sheep; He is the shepherd. Sheep do not attack a predator; they depend upon the shepherd for their protection. When we follow the Lord closely, He will be our defense. There is no greater protection from the demonic than the presence of the divine. We have no proper motivation for wanting to forsake our role of following as sheep and turn to fighting as soldiers.

The devil has been defeated, everything he does disintegrates at the presence of Jesus, and his doom was sealed in Heaven long before the creation of mankind. Christ is now leading His Church into green pastures to feed, breed, and relish the life He has given, and He will continue to protect us.

Christ's strategy toward individual believers is to indwell them. Not one of us is asked to live the Christian life. We are invited to let Christ live His life through us. What a difference! Our challenge is to maintain faith. If there is a conflict, it is to *"fight the good fight of faith"* (1 Timothy 6:12).

Our task is not to defeat Satan; our task is to consistently believe that Jesus completely defeated Satan. If we will listen to the voice of the indwelling Christ, He will remind us of the victory of Calvary.

Our responsibility is to obey the voice of Jesus within our hearts. He is in charge. We need to resist our gift of suspicion and believe the words of our Lord. When He says "fear not," it is futile to give in to our fears and charge the fortress of Satan. While fear may give us energy to act, it does not give us a corresponding ability. The ability to defeat the works of Satan consistently lies in the hands of Jesus Christ. If there is anything He needs for us to do, He will tell us. Until we receive such orders, we do well to rejoice in His presence, live in His grace, and rest in His love.

Chapter 8

Whose Mind Is It, Anyway?

For as he thinketh in his heart, so is he.
Proverbs 23:7

In looking at the various strategies involved in spiritual warfare, we have not yet looked at Satan's strategy. We may be certain that the devil's approach to war on the saints is vastly different from our technique of fighting him. Just as the confederate soldiers used guerilla tactics so dissimilar from the British soldiers marching in full rank that the small American force repeatedly defeated the larger British army, so Satan watches from behind trees as our formations advance in perfect rank and file. He doesn't fight us openly like we try to fight him.

The devil's battle plans do not call for an open confrontation in the heavens because he failed in that attempt in God's dwelling place. Neither does he want a direct confrontation with Christ, for he tried that at Calvary, and Jesus miserably defeated him at the very moment he thought he had triumphed.

Satan's battle stratagem is far more personal and individual. He fights for the minds of men and women, for he understands better than most Christians the power of the statement in the book of wisdom: *"For as he thinketh in his heart, so is he."* It does not say, "as he feeleth in his soul," for feelings seldom make radical changes in anyone. The governing force of life is the mind, and Satan has mastered the art of appealing to the thoughts of men and women.

Hitler and Stalin believed strongly in this principle. They knew that if they could capture the untrained minds of children and youth, they had that individual's life forever.

It is not by accident that the devil reaches so quickly for the minds of our youth, and it is tragic that so few parents realize how important it is to protect their children's eye and ear gates. If we allow our children to see and hear evil, or lust, or extreme pride, evil can become a governing principle throughout their lives—unless the power of the cross of Christ comes to liberate them later in life.

The devil also knows how susceptible we all are to visual and audio stimuli. Through television, the press, and the entertainment media, he introduces thought patterns that have the power to change the way we view life and the way we live it.

Satan works, for the most part, unseen and without the beating of drums or the blowing of trumpets. He conquers our minds with such pleasantness that we don't even know that we have been in a battle. He has the capacity to conquer a Christian without ever declaring war.

It is time for believers to wake up and realize that the conflict with Satan is not in the mystical heavens above us; it is in our minds. Our battle is less with spiritual forces outside us than it is with the beliefs, attitudes, and decisions they plant within us.

A review of the Sermon on the Mount shows no injunction to rise up and contend with forces in the atmosphere above. Jesus consistently admonishes us to change our thinking and our responses in life. The Beatitudes all call for a mental adjustment—sometimes requiring a one-hundred-and-eighty degree turn in our thinking.

One of Satan's constant inroads to our minds is worry. Without realizing that he likely has induced it, we allow anxiety and fear to dominate our thought patterns until they replace our peace with worry. Paul told the Christians in Philippi:

> *Be careful for nothing; but in every thing by prayer and supplication with thanksgiving let your requests be made known unto God. And the peace of God, which passeth all understanding, shall keep your hearts and minds through Christ Jesus. Finally, brethren, whatsoever things are true, whatsoever things are honest, whatsoever things are just, whatsoever things are pure, whatsoever things are lovely, whatsoever things are of good report, if there be any virtue, and if there be any praise, think on these things. Those things, which ye have both learned, and received, and heard, and seen in me, do: and the God of peace shall be with you.* Philippians 4:6-9

Paul was pleading with these Christians to win the battle of the mind.

The Mind Is the Seat of Life

So many things Jesus did illustrated deep spiritual

principles. Matthew and Mark both recorded an incident of a man in the country of the Gadarenes. This demonized man lived in the graveyards and was so ferocious that, although someone often chained and bound him with ropes, he broke every shackle. He became the object of fear in that countryside.

When Jesus landed on the shores of Gadara, this man approached Him and begged Him not to torment him. Jesus, however, had not come to torment the man. Instead of torment, Jesus released him from these fierce spirits and allowed them to go into a herd of swine on the hillside. The two thousand pigs couldn't stand demon possession and ran down a cliff into the sea and drowned. Understandably this caused a great outcry from the owners of the pigs. We read:

> *They come to Jesus, and see him that was possessed with the devil, and had the legion, sitting, and clothed, and in his right mind: and they were afraid.*
> Mark 5:15

Those who came to Jesus were amazed to see the formerly demonized man calm and clothed and rational. He was *"in his right mind."* The erratic behavior and the nudity disappeared when Christ restored the man's mind, as it always does. Releasing this man from some two thousand demons was not a difficult thing for Jesus. In doing it, He dealt with the demons where they were—in the man. The battleground was not outside the man, but inside him, and the thing that most amazed those who saw the change was the fact that the man was *"in his right mind."* That was the battleground.

Whose Mind Is It, Anyway?

The human mind is still the battlefield, for the mind is the seat of a person's life. The wise man wrote:

> *A sound heart is the life of the flesh: but envy the rottenness of the bones.* Proverbs 14:30

The contrast is striking: life or rottenness. The Hebrew word *leb* that is here translated as "heart" means "intellect." The Hebrews spoke of the heart as the seat of thought and will, while we speak of the mind as the seat of intelligence and reason. What Solomon had observed was that the thoughts of the heart (mind) control the nature of one's life. He wrote:

> *For as he thinketh in his heart, so is he.*
> Proverbs 23:7

God has not designed men and women to live in the emotions of their lives nor in the passionate appetites of their bodies. He has given us a superior intellect to every other creature on this Earth. We need not live according to basic instinct, for we have a mind that should rule the impulse and impetus of our minds and emotions.

One tragedy of drug use is the altering of the mind until the direction of the life is turned over to feeling and fantasy. Demon activity does a similar thing. It appeals to the intellect, seeking to gain control of the very seat of life of the individual.

A conspicuous difference between demon activity and divine activity through a person is that the demonic requires a mindless submission to an outside control, while the Holy Spirit always works cooperatively with the individual through whom He wishes to express Himself. The satanic consistently violates a person's mind and volitional freedom, while the Holy Spirit energizes a person without taking the intellect or free will away from him. Jesus said:

> *The thief cometh not, but for to steal, and to kill, and to destroy: I am come that they might have life, and that they might have it more abundantly.*
> John 10:10

Satan's desires are in sharp contrast to those of Jesus:

> *He was a murderer from the beginning, and abode not in the truth, because there is no truth in him. When he speaketh a lie, he speaketh of his own: for he is a liar, and the father of it.* John 8:44

Christ comes to the seat of our life to renew our minds, while Satan comes to fill our minds with lies and to murder what little life we may have left. This produces a battle in the brain, a struggle in the soul. Like it or not, our thought patterns direct life's activities.

The Mind Is the Source of Sin

While we would like to put the genesis of sin far outside of ourselves, the Scriptures teach that the source of sin is in the mind. Sin, of course, had its beginnings in Heaven when Satan exercised his will over the will of God. It was not his emotions that overcame Lucifer in Heaven. He deliberately set himself up as a replacement for God. It is unlikely that he did this in one giant step. His intellect progressively determined to unseat God in the heavens. His sin began as a thought, and the sin grew as the thought enlarged.

Similarly, in the Garden of Eden, Lucifer, in the form of the serpent, did not force Adam and Eve to sin. Satan simply convinced them that if they would disobey God and eat the forbidden fruit, they would become just like God (see Genesis 3:5). Like Lucifer in Heaven, the man and woman on Earth wanted an equality with God. Pride was rampant in their minds, and they schemed to achieve what their minds told them was available. Unwilling to wait for sufficient maturity and spiritual advancement, their minds sought a short cut, but what got cut was their intimate relationship with God.

The pattern of sin has not changed since then. At Iconium, Paul met with fierce opposition:

> *The unbelieving Jews stirred up the Gentiles, and made their minds evil affected against the brethren.*
>
> Acts 14:2

Paul and Barnabas were having a great revival in that city, but when the minds of the Gentile residents accepted evil reports, this godly team had to flee to Lystra to continue their ministry. This opposition was not the result of some great principality over Iconium. The sin was in the minds, not in the heavens. It was unbelieving Jews who infected the minds of the Gentiles, and their behavior reflected the change in their thinking.

Many teach that sin is an action, but the Word of God teaches that sin is an attitude. Technically a person is not a sinner because of what he does; a person does what he does because he is a sinner. Sin begins in the mind and awaits an opportunity for expression.

Jesus taught that sin begins with a thought. In the great Sermon on the Mount, He taught:

> *Ye have heard that it was said by them of old time, Thou shalt not commit adultery. I say unto you, that whosoever looketh on a woman to lust after her hath committed adultery with her already in his heart.* Matthew 5:27-28

Jesus showed that the deed was the expression of the desire. The sin of adultery begins in the intellect. It is a thought awaiting expression.

Even our judicial system recognizes that violent sin begins with a thought. The penalty for premeditated murder is far more severe than for involuntary manslaughter. Our courts have sentenced people to life in prison for contracting to have another person killed—even when the crime was not carried out. The court judged the desire as being as degenerate as the deed would have been.

It is a "cop-out" to say "The devil made me do it." It might be that the devil implanted the thought in the mind, but God does not judge us for passing thoughts. Our lives are directed by the lingering thoughts that build up desire and action.

The prophet understood that sin originates in the mind, for he wrote:

> *The sin of Judah is written with a pen of iron, and with the point of a diamond: it is graven upon the table of their heart.*
> *The heart is deceitful above all things, and desperately wicked: who can know it?*
>
> Jeremiah 17:1 and 9

The implication is that we don't even know the depravity of our own minds, for that is where sin is indelibly engraved.

Jesus clearly taught that sin has its origin in the minds of men and women when He said:

> *But those things which proceed out of the mouth come forth from the heart; and they defile the man. For out of the, heart proceed evil thoughts, murders, adulteries, fornications, thefts, false witness, blasphemies: these are the things that defile a man.*
>
> Matthew 15:18-20

These *"things"* that Jesus says are resident in the hearts of the unregenerate (and far too often even the redeemed) are the very things some try to pull down, cast out, or bind up. Little wonder they have no success, for they are exerting their energies in the wrong direction.

Perhaps what Peter told Simon the sorcerer, who tried to bribe Peter into giving him the power of the Holy Spirit, applies to all of us. Peter said:

> *Repent therefore of this thy wickedness, and pray God, if perhaps the thought of thine heart may be forgiven thee.* Acts 8:22

Some of the popularity of the current spiritual warfare teaching is that it allows people to project the sin in their own hearts to an unseen force beyond them. They can then condemn, judge, and vilify these sins without having to deal with them in their own hearts. Almost all of us want change, but few of us want change in ourselves. Like it or not, repentance, not rebuking, is God's provision for the removal of sin.

The Mind Is the Scene of the Battle

In his letter to the church in Rome, Paul declared:

> *And even as they did not like to retain God in their knowledge, God gave them over to a reprobate mind, to do those things which are not convenient.*
> Romans 1:28

Could God have said it any plainer? The battlefield is the mind. Those who will not discipline their minds to seek God are eventually released by God to fill their thoughts with whatever despicable, detestable, and disgraceful thing they may choose.

Six chapters later Paul admits that even following conversion there remained a war in his mind. He said:

> *But I see another law in my members, warring*

> *against the law of my mind, and bringing me into captivity to the law of sin which is in my members.*
> Romans 7:23

Paul did not speak of some principality over the city warring against the saints. He saw the conflict as being in his inner being. In the next chapter, he proclaimed:

> *The carnal mind is enmity against God: for it is not subject to the law of God, neither indeed can be. So then they that are in the flesh cannot please God.*
> Romans 8:7-8

If the mind is where we have warfare with the principles of righteousness, surely that is where we engage the powers of unrighteousness. It is an ideological warfare, and the weapons are words and ideas that desire to win over our thought patterns.

When we quote Paul's words, *"Casting down imaginations, and every high thing that exalteth itself against the knowledge of God,"* we must also complete the thought, *"and bringing into captivity every thought to the obedience of Christ." "Casting down imagination"* is not pulling down the strongholds over some geographic area; it is *"bringing into captivity every thought to the obedience of Christ."*

The subject of this chapter is Paul's defense of his ministry. Some in Corinth charged that Paul walked after the flesh. He assured them that *"Though we live in the world, we do not wage war as the world does"* (2 Corinthians 10:3, NIV). Having made tents for the Roman army, Paul was aware that warfare was conducted outside the soldier's life—even outside his encampment, whenever possible. In contrast to this, Paul pointed out that the Christian's war was inside himself—in the very center of his life. This prompted him to say:

> *The weapons we fight with are not the weapons of the world. On the contrary, they have divine power to demolish strongholds.*
>
> 2 Corinthians 10:4, NIV

Had Paul said no more, we might have to agree that the power God has given to us is to demolish satanic fortresses, but Paul continued his description of our warfare by writing:

> *Casting down imaginations, and every high thing that exalteth itself against the knowledge of God, and bringing into captivity every thought to the obedience of Christ.* 2 Corinthians 10:5

The New International Version translates this verse as:

> *We demolish arguments and every pretension that sets itself up against the knowledge of God, and we take captive every thought to make it obedient to Christ.*

The New American Standard Bible puts it this way:

> *We are destroying speculations and every lofty thing raised against the knowledge of God, and we*

> *are taking every thought captive to the obedience of Christ.*

Paul makes no allusions here to fighting high-level demonic forces in the heavens above him. He is declaring that his warfare was against the speculations, arguments, and prideful high thoughts that exalt themselves against God. His challenge was to *"take captive every thought to make it obedient to Christ."* Why? He knew that the true battle between godliness and ungodliness was in the minds of men and women. He warred to bring his thoughts into captivity to obey Christ, and so must we.

In his letter to the Ephesian Christians, Paul wrote:

> *So I tell you this, and insist on it in the LORD, that you must no longer live as the Gentiles do, in the futility of their thinking. They are darkened in their understanding and separated from the life of God because of the ignorance that is in them due to the hardening of their hearts. Having lost all sensitivity, they have given themselves over to sensuality so as to indulge in every kind of impurity, with a continual lust for more. You, however, did not come to know Christ that way. Surely you heard of him and were taught in him in accordance with the truth that is in Jesus. You were taught, with regard to your former way of life, to put off your old self, which is being corrupted by its deceitful desires, to be made new in the attitude of your minds, and to put on the new self, created to be like God in true righteousness and holiness.* Ephesians 4:17-24, NIV

Since the battleground is our minds, we can expect the enemy to attack us there. Accordingly, Peter urges us:

> *Wherefore gird up the loins of your mind, be sober, and hope to the end for the grace that is to be brought unto you at the revelation of Jesus Christ.*
> 1 Peter 1:13

Rather than concentrate on Satan in the sky, we would do well to join David in pleading to God in Heaven:

> *Create in me a clean heart, O God; and renew a right spirit within me.* Psalm 51:10

THE MIND IS THE SUBJECT OF CHRIST'S RENEWAL

Any student of the Word of God must come to the conclusion that the mind is the standard by which God judges a man. He judges the thoughts and attitudes of every individual. Since motivations are more important to God than manifestations, He searches the heart and mind and judges us accordingly. He told His chosen people, Israel:

> *I know the things that come into your mind, every one of them.* Ezekiel 11:5

> *I the LORD search the heart, I try the reins, even to give every man according to his ways, and according to the fruit of his doings.* Jeremiah 17:10

Surely, then, the mind is where God passes sentence. God judges us according to our thoughts, not our words, for our words often conceal more than they reveal. God knows what is in our minds and responds to us accordingly.

Because God knows that the mind is the battlefield where we engage the enemy in conflict, He promised:

> *For this is the covenant that I will make with the house of Israel after those days, saith the Lord; I will put my laws into their mind, and write them in their hearts: and I will be to them a God, and they shall be to me a people.* Hebrews 8:10

Our major weapon against temptation and the tempter is the Word of God, so the Lord promised to put His Word in our minds. Rather than REBUKE, we need but remember and rehearse the wonderful Word God has imparted into our minds and spirits. Instead of spending our worship time inducing an attitude of warfare, we would do better to remember and apply the precious promise:

> *Thou wilt keep him in perfect peace, whose mind is stayed on thee: because he trusteth in thee.*
> Isaiah 26:3

Contention and strife, even if we direct it against the devil, are counterproductive to the worship of God.

It seems impractical, if not impossible, to fight against the kingdom of darkness while trying to worship the God of light. They dwell in incompatible kingdoms, and do not even share the same phone line. So if you are talking to the devil and wish to speak to God, hang up and redial. The reverse is equally true. God and the devil will not accept conference calls. You can speak to only one of them at a time.

The martyrs in Heaven admitted that they did not overcome Satan by directly confronting him:

> *They overcame him by the blood of the Lamb, and by the word of their testimony.* Revelation 12:11

We need to rely far more on the finished work of Christ instead of continually trying to finish His work for Him.

In speaking of the reconciling work of Christ Jesus, Paul wrote:

> *Once you were alienated from God and were enemies in your minds because of* [margin note: "as shown by"] *your evil behavior. But now he has reconciled you by Christ's physical body through death to present you holy in his sight, without blemish and free from accusation.*
>
> Colossians 1:21-22, NIV

One work of the cross of Christ was to change our thinking, for when we change our minds, our behavior changes. Christ's work of reconciliation makes it possible for us to be renewed:

> *Be renewed in the spirit of your mind.*
>
> Ephesians 4:23

Whose Mind Is It, Anyway?

Be not conformed to this world: but be ye transformed by the renewing of your mind, that ye may prove what is that good, and acceptable, and perfect, will of God. Romans 12:2

This need for a changed mind is not fulfilled by mere exercise. It is far more a matter of exchange. The New Testament urges us:

Let this mind be in you, which was also in Christ Jesus. Philippians 2:5

Knowing the impossibility of totally changing a reprobate mind, God invites us to trade our mind-set for the mind-set of Jesus. He had learned to delight in doing the will of God (see Psalm 40:8).

We need not await entering eternity to have this change of mind, for the promise of the Word is:

For God hath...given us...a sound mind.
2 Timothy 1:7

We have the mind of Christ. 1 Corinthians 2:16

What a great promise! *"We have the mind of Christ!"* That means we don't think as we once thought. We are able to think with His thoughts. We need to remind ourselves that Jesus thinks He has defeated the devil. He has promised:

We are more than conquerors through him that loved us. Romans 8:37

The context of this promise is a listing of forces that might try to separate us from the love of God that is in Christ Jesus. The New American Standard Bible translation puts it like this:

> *But in all these things we overwhelmingly conquer through Him who loved us.*

This is the way Jesus thinks about our conflicts here. He has conquered every enemy that could array itself against us. We need not go to such great lengths to redo His completed work. We merely need to see the conflict as He sees it.

It is good that God has a sense of humor, or His judgment would fail to satiate His anger. In one of our American Christian magazines, I saw an advertisement purchased by an entrepreneur who was leasing a Boeing 747 to take Christian soldiers up to a height of 35,000 feet to better engage in pulling down the "high places" of the devil. Charter seats were available for sale. This same man also advertised that he was renting the top floors of the tallest buildings in our major cities for those who wanted to engage in conflict with the high spiritual forces. What difference does altitude make? Still, people paid good money to ascend into the heights to do spiritual warfare with Satan.

We have the mind of Christ, and such foolishness should not appeal to us. The spiritual battle that Christ enjoined with Satan was here on the Earth, and He defeated the devil in the wilderness, in the garden, and on the cross. He knows that Satan was defeated in Heaven, for He watched as Michael threw Lucifer out.

Jesus also knows that Satan is defeated on the Earth, for He was the one who defeated him.

We need to let the mind of Christ work in our minds. He isn't interested in shadow boxing, nor will He join us in mock battles with a defeated opponent. We need to have a change of mind about these pseudo-spiritual activities and let the mind of Christ direct our thoughts to the worship of God. While many now allow Christian leaders to direct their thoughts to Satan and his position of power, Paul prayed:

> *The Lord direct your hearts into the love of God, and into the patient waiting for Christ.*
>
> 2 Thessalonians 3:5

Some have been so brainwashed in this matter of spiritual warfare that they live in a constant fighting mode. May the Holy Spirit communicate to them that Christ has provided a renewal of their minds. They need not live in a mind-set of war. They can enjoy peace and tranquility while still alive on this Earth.

Whose mind is it, anyway? Should we be guided by the mind of man trying to lead a congregation into a battle against high demonic forces, or should we be guided by the mind of Christ that says the battle has already been won?

Chapter 9

Whose Victory Is It, Anyway?

They sung a new song, saying, Thou art worthy to take the book, and to open the seals thereof: for thou wast slain, and hast redeemed us to God by thy blood out of every kindred, and tongue, and people, and nation. Revelation 5:9

I live in Phoenix, Arizona, home of the Cardinals—a professional football team that hasn't had a winning season in many years. Almost every professional football team in America likes to play the Cardinals, for they believe they will likely win. Our team generates a lot of sympathy, but wins few games and receive no awards.

I find it interesting the way the sportswriters and television sportscasters can make our team sound so good just before a game. They try to make us believe that the team has had a turnaround and will definitely win this time. Unfortunately, it usually proves to be just more "hype," and our team loses, often by a narrow margin.

I feel sorry for our team, but not sorry enough to bother to go to the stadium and watch them play. Sometimes I think we should have moments when we are sorry for the devil, for he, like the Arizona Cardinals, never has a winning season. He boasts a lot but produces little or nothing. Occasionally the devil can make a weak Christian believe that he (the devil) will win the next contest, but he seldom does. He usually loses. The devil is a loser, and he lacks the ability to have a winning season with the Church as a whole.

Some of our preachers remind me of the sportscasters in Phoenix who consistently predict a victory in the next contest. They fill their sermons with random facts and statistics. They wrest scripture verses out of their settings to prove that the devil is winning against the Church. They draw a good attendance, but they're always wrong. The devil never wins.

If Satan has never won in the six thousand years of Bible history, why are we afraid he will win now? I know that it is popular to say that things are worse in the world now than at any other time, and perhaps they are. Since I have never lived in another generation, I have no personal point of comparison to help me determine whether or not it is true. In reading the writings of men in the seventeenth and eighteenth centuries, however, it impresses me to see that they said that things were worse in their generation than at any other time in history. Perhaps everyone is right. Maybe there is a progressive degeneration in humanity, but if this proves to be true, it is the result of sin in people and not because Satan is winning a battle in the heavens above us.

In the closing days of the twentieth century, we certainly have the potential for greater degeneracy than at any other time. There are more persons alive on this Earth now than at any other period in the history of humanity. Also, because of our modern means of communication and rapid transportation, we can be more sinful, in more places, and in more ways than ever before. Communications also lets us know what others are doing and shows us how to sin as they are sinning.

None of this indicates, in any way, that Satan and his kingdom are winning. He still has the same goals—to unseat God and replace Him, but he has not achieved it until now, and he never will.

Two or three times a year our football team wins a game—often against some league leader who has became overconfident. This does nothing to advance our team in the long term, although it can ruin the chances of the other team to advance in divisional rankings. Satan, much like our Arizona Cardinals, is a spoiler. Occasionally he can spoil another's chances for success, but he, himself, cannot succeed.

Satan is a victim, not a victor. He has been so completely conquered that he can never be a conqueror. Like the man who has allowed alcohol to defeat him, Satan will brag to anyone who will listen, but he is too degenerate to do ten percent of what he claims he can do.

Satan has never won a victory

I dare not claim that Satan has never won a skirmish. Even our hardluck Arizona Cardinals occasionally win a game, but a win or two does not make a champion. Satan sometimes finds a weak lamb or a straggling sheep separated from the flock and makes a kill, but this does not make him the leader of the flock. His tactics may prevent a local church congregation from achieving its goals in a given situation, but that is not a true victory, only a momentary setback. If the congregation returns to prayer, it will recover the ground lost and eventually achieve its goals.

There are three areas where Satan has fought hard and lost. He fought God for *position,* he fights humanity for *souls,* and he fights the Church for *power.* His fight for position began in God's Heaven where he was the anointed cherub that covered the ark. God exalted him above every being He had created, but Lucifer was not content. He wanted God's position. Five times he lifted himself in pride to cry loudly into eternity, "I will...." He seems to have succeeded in winning the allegiance of at least one-third of the angels in Heaven, but when they made their claims of superiority to Almighty God, Lucifer heard God refuse to fight with him directly. How humiliating! As we have seen, God merely commissioned an angel of lower rank to throw Lucifer and his angels out of Heaven.

Satan did not win anything in this battle. He lost his position as archangel, his place in God's presence, and his power as second only to God Himself. Michael, at God's command, cast him out of Heaven and down to Earth. He lost his name, and, at the ascension of Christ, he lost every title he had convinced men he still possessed.

God allowed Satan to exercise his will, but He did not allow him to execute that will. He can boast about his aspirations, but he cannot bring those ambitions into being. He is a fired executive who unsuccessfully sued for reinstatement.

Satan is just as unsuccessful in maintaining control

over the souls of men on this Earth. He seems to have reasoned that if he could control God's special creatures, he could outvote God and still meet his original goal of replacing Him. Calvary nullified this strategy.

It is not that Satan is unable to get control of people. History shows too conclusively how well he can control a Hitler or a Stalin. He used them for mass murder and to exert political control over many nations. If Satan hoped to gain control of the Earth through these people, however, he miscalculated, for at the moment of their individual deaths, Satan lost their influence and service.

The kingdom of Satan can work only on and through the living. The dead are of no use to him. Contrariwise, once an individual gives his or her allegiance to Jesus, he or she is His eternally. Paul speaks of *"the whole family in heaven and earth"* (Ephesians 3:15). God has one family, some of whom live and serve Him on Earth, and the rest of whom live and serve Him in Heaven. Death does not separate the Christian from the family of God; it merely changes his location. How Satan must wish he had the same structure in his kingdom!

Satan's third front in his war has been against the Church. God gave to the Church the relationship with Him and the divine energy that Satan lost when he was exiled from Heaven, and Satan earnestly wants to regain this. No price seems too great to him. Consistently Satan has infiltrated the Church, especially at leadership levels, but just as consistently, Christ has raised new divisions in His Church that resist such infiltration. Jesus implied that the devil sows tares in the wheat fields of the Church, but God commissions angels to go through those fields to pull out the tares. God does not prevent Satan from coming against the Church; He merely prevents him from defeating the Church.

One of the devil's most powerful tools against the Church has been the threat of death. Through the centuries, and even in modern times, millions of believers have been martyred by agents of Satan. The devil seems to believe that if he can kill the faithful, he can control the less zealous. But he is wrong again! History reveals that the blood of the martyrs has always been the seed of the Church. The Church has grown stronger and larger whenever the devil starts his death marches.

How disheartening it must be to Satan to hear the testimony in Heaven that the martyrs *"overcame him by the blood of the Lamb, and by the word of their testimony."* Satan did not overcome these saints; they overcame him. He did not triumph over them; he merely transferred them into Heaven.

Satan seeks to control people with fear and loathing, but Jesus controls men and women through faith and love. Fox's *Book of Martyrs,* which chronicles the severe torture of men and women for their faith in past centuries, tells of hundreds of spectators who witnessed the martyr's bravery in death and gave their own lives to Christ Jesus to replace martyred believers. Even when it appeared that the devil had gained supremacy, he lost, for love is always more powerful than hatred.

JESUS HAS NEVER LOST A CONFLICT

In his insurrection against God, Satan has been frustrated because God has never directly engaged him in conflict. In Heaven, it was angel against angel, and on Earth, the conflict is devil against man. God has forced Satan to contend with persons far beneath the Almighty, and Satan can't even win the battle with them.

Lacking opportunity to fight God directly, Satan focused himself to combat three of God's special loves:

1. His special creation—Adam and Eve
2. His special family—Israel
3. His special Son—Jesus, the Christ

In each of these conflicts our God was victorious.

Satan was quick to pounce angrily on God's special creation. When God created Adam and Eve as a replacement for Lucifer (who had been the special object of God's love), the devil sought to destroy the relationship between God and His new love objects. Entering the garden as a serpent, he tempted them to disobedience by appealing to their pride and vanity. It appeared that he succeeded, for the man and the woman lost the covering of the glory of God and came under God's curse.

Before Satan could organize a celebration party, however, God slew innocent animals and used their skins to make coats to cover the nakedness of Adam and Eve. By God's choice, this shedding of the blood of the innocent renewed Adam and Eve to fellowship with Him. Although driven from the Garden, God preserved their way to the Tree of Life, and they learned to approach God through sacrifices on the altar. Satan, who thought he had won the game, discovered that he had simply made a touchdown. Jesus won the contest in the Garden of Eden, for He became our substitute Lamb, taking upon Himself the death each of us deserve. In Heaven, we hear the testimony: *"Thou art worthy...for thou...hast redeemed us to God by thy blood out of every kindred, and tongue, and people, and nation."*

GOD'S SPECIAL FAMILY ATTACKED

The second object of God's love that Satan attacked was God's special family. When God chose a special family through Abraham, Satan sought to frustrate His purposes. The devil enslaved the members of that family when they went to Egypt to escape a famine he produced, but God delivered them with great signs and wonders and brought them back to the land God had given to Abraham.

Satan inspired many different nations to war against Israel, but God consistently delivered His people from their hands. The most notable of these was the work of enraged Nebuchadnezzar when he finally captured Jerusalem and took many of its inhabitants back to Babylon with him. It is likely that the devil announced to his troops that he had finally found a man who could help him win a war, but God called Nebuchadnezzar *"My servant"* (Jeremiah 27:6).

Because God raised up Nebuchadnezzar, He had the authority to put him down. Seventy years later, God moved upon the kings who conquered Babylon to release the Jews to return to their homeland. No opposition that Satan could raise against their return or their reconstruction of the Temple and the city of

Jerusalem succeeded. God caused every resistance to turn to the benefit of the returned Jews. It was an Old Testament example of the New Testament promise:

> *All things work together for good to them that love God, to them who are the called according to his purpose.* Romans 8:28

God's Special Son Attacked

The third object of Satan's wicked wrath was God's special Son, Jesus Christ. An inspired Paul tells us:

> *But when the fulness of the time was come, God sent forth his Son, made of a woman, made under the law, To redeem them that were under the law, that we might receive the adoption of sons.*
> Galatians 4:4-5

This seemed to be the devil's first chance to fight directly with God, for Jesus was God made flesh. Seeking an early win, Satan made a play to kill Jesus in His infancy, but he failed. Had he known what the shepherds knew or the non-covenant wise men learned, he might have had a better chance. The angels, however, so completely hid Christ's birth from the devil that he did not seem to learn of it until the wise men visited Herod and openly asked questions about this birth. Satan clearly doesn't know everything. He is simply a good listener.

The slaughter of the children in Bethlehem from three years of age and under was a waste of life, for God had already directed Joseph to take Mary and Jesus to Egypt for safety. Again, the devil did not know of this. His intelligence service failed him miserably, as it often does. Even his great host of demons do not know everything that is transpiring around them. Before Satan could locate Jesus, John the Baptist was already baptizing Him in the Jordan River. God spoke His approval of His son, and the Holy Spirit descended in the form of a dove and rested on Jesus in an anointing of ordination for service.

Satan discovered this and followed Jesus into the wilderness to tempt Him. He waited until Christ was weary and hungry from a forty-day fast, and then he made his best offer. When no amount of pressure could change Jesus' mind, the devil realized that he had lost the battle:

> *And when the devil had ended all the temptation, he departed from him for a season.* Luke 4:13

Again Jesus triumphed over the devil.

Throughout Christ's ministry, the devil sought to destroy Him. He produced a severe storm on the Sea of Galilee when Jesus was asleep in the boat. It should have swamped the boat and destroyed Jesus and His disciples, but Jesus stood up and rebuked the storm, producing a calm. Jesus had won again!

When Jesus visited His hometown of Nazareth and taught in the synagogue, there was a violent response:

> *All they in the synagogue, when they heard these things, were filled with wrath, And rose up, and*

thrust him out of the city, and led him unto the brow of the hill whereon their city was built, that they might cast him down headlong.

Luke 4:28-29

Angels must have closed the eyes of the people that day, for no one was able to lay a hand on Jesus. Score another victory for Him!

Angry men and women—from religious leaders to pig owners—repeatedly sought to do Christ physical harm, but they could not touch Him. Jesus even got away with overturning the tables of the money changers and releasing the sacrificial animals for sale in the Temple. He was untouchable, invincible. He won every confrontation He entered.

Having lost every raid against Jesus, Satan gambled his entire army in a frontal assault against God's Son in the crucifixion. It made sense to him and his counselors to risk everything to kill Jesus. They were amazed at how easily they succeeded. Jesus always seemed to be in the right place at the right time, saying the right things. His capture in the garden was made easier through the help of Judas. His trial didn't take long, because Jesus didn't enter a defense, preferring to remain silent. When the soldiers drove the square iron spikes through the hands and feet of Jesus and then hoisted that crude cross into the air, all Hell began a victory celebration that rivaled the coronation of a monarch. Satan bragged that God had made a serious tactical error in sending His Son to become a man who could die.

While the hosts of Satan rejoiced at their amazing

victory, all Heaven rejoiced that Satan had played into the hands of God. They knew that Satan had been unable to do one thing outside the perfect will of God for His Son and their plan of redemption. On the day of Pentecost, Peter preached:

> *Him, being delivered by the determinate counsel and foreknowledge of God, ye have taken, and by wicked hands have crucified and slain.* Acts 2:23

Every step of the arrest, trial, crucifixion, and burial of Jesus was consistent with the predetermined will of God Who foreknew everything that was to be done. Then one of God's couriers interrupted Satan's victory celebration with the message: "Jesus is risen!" Even the grave could not contain Him, and this meant absolute defeat for Satan—in the midst of apparent victory. Once again, Jesus wins!

There still has not been a direct confrontation between Satan and God. Even at Calvary, Satan was confronting the God/man, but Jesus has been successful in every confrontation the devil has initiated.

Jesus will always win over Satan, for Christ is far more qualified to work through people than is the devil. Jesus knows all things, and, in comparison, the devil has very limited knowledge. Our enemy has limited power, and even more limited permission to use that power, while our Lord said of Himself:

> *All power is given unto me in heaven and in earth.*
> Matthew 28:18

Whose Victory Is It, Anyway?

The great songwriters of Israel saw the perpetual victory of the Lord. They wrote:

> *Thine, O LORD, is the greatness, and the power, and the glory, and the victory, and the majesty: for all that is in the heaven and in the earth is thine; thine is the kingdom, O LORD, and thou art exalted as head above all.* 1 Chronicles 29:11

> *O sing unto the LORD a new song, for he hath done marvelous things: his right hand, and his holy arm, hath gotten him the victory.* Psalm 98:1

Jesus has not only consistently defeated the devil in every confrontation, but He will continue to defeat the devil up to the day He casts him into the Lake of Fire. Why, then, should we Christians get so worked up in trying to defeat an opponent who has already lost the battle?

BELIEVERS TRIUMPH IN CHRIST

Satan is a proven loser. He makes an occasional good play, but he cannot win the game. At Calvary, Jesus testified: *"It is finished"* (John 19:30). It was as though Jesus had said, "I have run up such a lead in this game that Satan cannot win, even if he makes a touchdown every hour on the hour until I return. We win! Let's put in the scrub team (the Church) and let them get some practice." We may get to play in this game of life, but we cannot lose, for Christ assured victory in the game before He sent us in.

Collectively believers form the Church on Earth and in Heaven. Jesus said of that Church:

> *I say also unto thee, That thou art Peter, and upon this rock I will build my church; and the gates of hell shall not prevail against it.* Matthew 16:18

Peter had just made his great testimony of faith in declaring *"Thou art the Christ, the son of the living God"* (Matthew 16:16). Jesus now said He would build His Church on such a confession and that the gates of Hell would not prevail against it.

Some preachers use this verse to say that Satan cannot hide in a walled city, for we are authorized to pull the gates of the city off its hinges and go in to conquer him. Perhaps—but that is taking the verse way out of context. Jesus was talking about building His church, not about charging an enemy fortress. Within the gates of ancient cities was where the elders of the city transacted their business. "The gates," therefore, were the equivalent of today's city hall. What Jesus said here is that when He is building His Church, there is not enough power, even in Hell itself, to prevent Him from completing His task. No legal maneuvers, however clever, can hinder His purposes.

Legal and political systems have repeatedly sought to stop the spread of the Gospel. They sometimes have limited success, but they eventually fail. There is a divine law that so supersedes human law that Heaven acts as a Supreme Court overturning the rulings of earthly magistrates, when it affects the development of Christ's Church on Earth. *"The gates ...shall not prevail against it."*

In a different language, but with similar meaning, the New Testament further assures us:

> *That at the name of Jesus every knee should bow, of things in Heaven, and things in earth, and things under the earth; And that every tongue should confess that Jesus Christ is* L*ORD, to the glory of God the Father.* Philippians 2:10-11

Collectively and individually, believers are triumphant. The battle is over, and we win in Christ! Paul declared a present reality:

> *We are more than conquerors through him that loved us.* Romans 8:37

As *"more than conquerors,"* we are like an occupation army enforcing the terms of surrender. We are not fighting, but our very presence executes Christ's authority. The psalmist says this is one of the effects of praise:

> *Let the high praises of God be in their mouth, and a two-edged sword in their hand; To execute vengeance upon the heathen, and punishments upon the people; To bind their kings with chains, and their nobles with fetters of iron; To execute upon them the judgment written. This honour have all his saints. Praise ye the* L*ORD.* Psalm 149:6-9

Our pure worship of God enforces His terms of victory over the devil. We *"are more than conquerors."* Our role in this life is not to conquer territory for Christ; He has already conquered that territory for us. Our role is to accept and live in that victory.

Not only do collective believers, the Church, enjoy victory over Satan; individual believers are equally assured that what Jesus did to the devil is applicable to their personal lives. John the Beloved wrote:

> *For whatsoever is born of God overcometh the world: and this is the victory that overcometh the world, even our faith.* 1 John 5:4

Overcoming is a very personal matter. Our most powerful God-given weapon, the one that overcomes everything the devil can bring against us in this world, is faith in Christ's finished work, as declared in God's Word.

Personal faith in Jesus is what God desires from us, not fighting to finish the work for God. The triumph believers enjoy in life is not because of a victory they have personally won over their enemy. Ours is a triumph of rejoicing in the victory Jesus gained for us. Our victory is a gift given, not a glory gained.

Christian believers not only triumph with Christ in life; we equally triumph with Him in death. Christ conquered our last enemy—death—when He died in our place. Although He has not yet abolished death, He has fully conquered it. Paul said of the living Christ after His resurrection:

> *For he must reign, till he hath put all enemies un-*

der his feet. The last enemy that shall be destroyed is death. For he hath put all things under his feet.
1 Corinthians 15:25-27

Paul also shared this conviction:

To be absent from the body [is] *to be present with the Lord.* 2 Corinthians 5:8

When Satan holds the scepter of death over us as a threat, he finds no fear response in us, for the worst that death can do to us is to transfer us immediately into the presence of the living God. Therefore blood-bought saints can stare death in the face and shout:

O death, where is thy sting? O grave, where is thy victory? The sting of death is sin; and the strength of sin is the law. But thanks be to God, which giveth us the victory through our Lord Jesus Christ.
1 Corinthians 15:55-57

We can stand by the casket of our loved ones and know that they are in the presence of the Lord. We take comfort in the knowledge that when Christ returns the second time, He will abolish death. The grave will open, and our departed loved one will enjoy the reuniting of body with the soul and spirit. The prophet saw this long before Jesus came. He wrote:

He will swallow up death in victory, and the LORD *God will wipe away tears from off all faces, and the rebuke of his people shall he take away from off all the earth: for the* LORD *hath spoken it.*

Isaiah 25:8

Even in death, we triumph in Christ, and Satan loses.

CHRIST WILL ENFORCE HIS VICTORY OVER SATAN

Although Jesus completely defeated Satan, He did not remove him from the Earth. Satan was allowed to retain his kingdom for a short season, but it is a very restricted, controlled kingdom. Christ more than declared its end; He showed it in the final revelation. John wrote:

I saw an angel come down from Heaven, having the key of the bottomless pit and a great chain in his hand. And he laid hold on the dragon, that old serpent, which is the Devil, and Satan, and bound him a thousand years, And cast him into the bottomless pit, and shut him up, and set a seal upon him, that he should deceive the nations no more, till the thousand years should be fulfilled: and after that he must be loosed a little season. Revelation 20:1-3

Following Christ's Second Coming, the nations of the Earth will be freed from the deception Satan likes to induce, and we, the saints, will join Christ in ruling the Earth in righteousness. After this predetermined period, Satan will be released from the Pit and will cause such deception in men and women that they will join him in a frontal assault upon God and His saints. This vast army will be destroyed with fire that comes down from Heaven to devour them (see Revelation 20:9), but a worse fate is reserved for Satan. We read:

> *And the devil that deceived them was cast into the lake of fire and brimstone, where the beast and the false prophet are, and shall be tormented day and night forever and ever.* Revelation 20:10

This is the last we hear of the devil in the Scriptures. He is not annihilated; he will be perpetually tormented in the Lake of Fire. Christ's victories over Satan are eternal.

Satan's domain is impounded, his dominion is restricted, his dominance is curtailed, and his doom is sealed. Why do we fear him so? Why do we feel we must enforce upon him something that Christ has not yet enforced?

God did not redeem us to communicate with the devil. Christ died to reconcile us to fellowship with God, not to fellowship with a fallen devil. Unless he makes a frontal attack on us, we do well to leave him alone. Deal with God. Talk to God. If we do the works that God has sent us to do, we will not have time or energy to be playing war with the devil.

CHAPTER 10

WHOSE WORSHIP IS IT, ANYWAY?

But the hour cometh, and now is, when the true worshippers shall worship the Father in spirit and in truth: for the Father seeketh such to worship him.

John 4:23

There is much speculation about where the Church is on the prophetic time clock as we enter into the twenty-first century. There are, of course, many who boldly proclaim that we have reached the end of time. One of the most visible American television speakers recently proclaimed on his broadcast that we now have only two years before the return of Jesus. Many others just like him are making us freshly aware of the nearness of the coming of Christ.

Personally, I hope they are right, but I do not know when Jesus will return. My grandfather, who was a preacher, told me that when his generation reached the end of the last century, many proclaimed that it was the end of the world and that Jesus would come immediately. They were obviously wrong in that assumption.

I know that I will go to be with Christ when He returns for His saints, but when exactly that will be I cannot say. There is, however, one thing of which I am certain. We have, in this past decade, come into the age of which Jesus spoke to the woman at Jacob's well. Christ's "now is" hour of worship has arrived, and across the United States and throughout the world, congregations have become vibrant with vocal and physical expressions of worship.

Most church congregations now have a worship leader backed by a special singing group. The immediate goal is to involve the people in a worship experience instead of letting them observe the choir, the organist, or a soloist performing. In many of these groups, the overhead projector has replaced the hymnals, the piano and organ have given way to keyboards, guitars, and trumpets, and contemporary melodies have supplanted the music of Bach as worshipers are lost in simple choruses of praise and adoration to the Lord.

There have always been worshipers of God, but it is unlikely that any society ever saw so many worshipers involved in praising the Lord as in our present generation. This explosion of praise has not been confined to Charismatic circles. It has crossed theological lines, invading the historic denominations and forming the hub of the latest religious groups to come on the scene. This is a wonderful time to be a Christian!

It is popular to seek reasons for this explosion of worship in our generation, and I cannot resist the temptation to join in this search. I find three reasons are nearly self-evident:

1. God created praise as part of human nature.
2. The Spirit commanded praise in the Bible.
3. Jesus certified praise to be a continuing practice.

Lest we become proud in thinking that we have discovered something lost to the Church of Jesus Christ, we need to remind ourselves that the issue has not been to convince people to worship; everyone worships. It is inherent in our natures to worship, for God programmed worship into the intrinsic personality of Adam and Eve, and they passed it on to their progeny. Cain and Able worshiped, and it was the difference in their manner of worship that produced the contention between them.

Everyone is a worshiper of something or someone. It may be God or it may be a star in sports or entertainment or even a leader in religion. Worship is not always directed toward a person. Sometimes people worship feelings (characteristic of drug users) and, at other times, people worship possessions, positions, or power. Interestingly enough, I was recently in Toronto, Canada, and read the banner headline for a story in one of their newspapers. It said: "THE HIGH PRIESTS OF MONEY MINISTER BEFORE THEIR CONGREGATIONS TODAY." The story was about bankers meeting with their shareholders. Even the unconverted see an analogy between the love of money and worship.

No, today's Christians have not discovered something new. Worship is part of the dynamics of the human spirit. What we have done is to direct this energetic public release as a response to God.

This new style of reaction to God has been blessed by the assistance of worship symposiums and conferences. Qualified musicians have taught others how to flow in worship on their instruments and in their singing. Artists have instructed lay men and women how to construct beautiful banners, and dancers have both demonstrated and taught the use of body language in worshiping God.

I seriously doubt if there has ever been a generation of believers who were better informed in the art of worship. I fear, however, that while we have learned to praise gloriously, we may have unwittingly departed from the object of worship whom Jesus told the Samaritan woman would be the recipient of our adoration. He said that *"true worshippers shall worship the Father."*

Worship Defined

The biblical teaching on worship does not begin in the Psalter. The Holy Spirit has impregnated every division of our Bible with descriptions, delineations, and demarcations for worship. The historic books, the books of poetry, the prophetic books, the Gospels, the Epistles, and the final book of Revelation all demand worship, detail worship, direct worship, and demonstrate worship. While we have no verse in scripture that says, "Worship of God is...," the examples that the Bible gives demonstrate that worship is the outpouring of an inner attitude toward God. It is exaggerative love that is enthusiastically expressed to God. My favorite definition of worship is: "Worship is love responding to love."

The Bible consistently demonstrates worship as a physical expression of an emotional attitude. Worship is always more than an attitude; it is an attitude expressed to God. Worship is the presenting of a thought or feeling to God in a positive, reverential manner. We may give it in a praise, a prayer, or a psalm. We may express it by physical actions or by words. We may accompany it with a gift, or the worship itself may be our gift to God.

The New Testament recognizes our weakness in releasing worship to God, so it promises the assistance of the Holy Spirit who indwells believers. In His discourse on worship to the Samaritan woman at Jacob's well, Jesus continued:

> *God is a Spirit: and they that worship him must worship him in spirit and in truth.* John 4:24

While this is both a definition and a regulation of our worship, it is also an astute assurance of the help of the Spirit, for in the preceding verse Jesus had declared that *"true worshipers shall worship the Father in spirit and in truth."* This is more than a prophecy; it is a statement of Christ's provision. When Jesus ascended, the Holy Spirit descended to replace Christ's presence in believers, and the Holy Spirit is a superb worshiper. When we allow Him to do so, He worships God through us in a marvelous manner. Even the gifts of the Spirit are tools that enrich our worship responses to God.

In seeking to encourage the Gentile believers to realize that they were as much in the covenant promises as Israel, Paul wrote:

> *For we are the circumcision, which worship God in the spirit, and rejoice in Christ Jesus, and have no confidence in the flesh.* Philippians 3:3

Paul said that it was not the outward rite of circumcision that determined who were God's chosen people; worshipers are God's covenant people.

In this verse, Paul tells us four things about New

Testament worship. First, it is directed to God: *"which worship God."* The Bible calls all worship directed to anyone other than God "idolatry." Worship must be deliberately directed to God to be accepted by Him. Talking to Satan can never be accepted as worship of God.

Second, we worship *"in the spirit."* Worship is expressed through the mind and body of the worshiper, but true worship comes from the inner being. In speaking of the coming Holy Spirit, Jesus said:

> *He that believeth on me, as the scripture hath said, out of his belly shall flow rivers of living water.*
>
> John 7:38

God's Spirit dwells in our spirits, and when we release Him in worship, that release is in our spirits.

Third, worship always responds with rejoicing *"in Christ Jesus,"* and anytime we lose our rejoicing, we automatically lose our worship.

Fourth, worship is not a fleshly activity: *"have no confidence in the flesh."* Worship is more than an act of the mind. It is far more than a physical demonstration. Worship flows through the spirit, aided by the Holy Spirit, with the mind and body giving expression to our rejoicing in the spirit. If what we purport to do as worship is only a fleshly demonstration, it does not qualify.

Worship may be expressed in dancing, singing, shouting, or playing musical instruments, but all of those things can be done without it being worship. It is the correlation and contrast between cause and effect. The cause of worship is rejoicing produced by the indwelling Spirit of God, and its effect may be extremely varied. Just doing what we did when worship was flowing in the past cannot be classified as worship, for repeating an effect cannot restore the worship. True worship starts within a person, is aided by the Holy Spirit, and is expressed to God with rejoicing in Christ Jesus. We can never accomplish this with mere fleshly activities. Like the light bulb that gives no light until its inner core becomes energized with electricity, so we cannot worship God until the power of the Holy Spirit energizes our inner spirits.

Worship Demanded

It is unlikely that the Bible commands anything more frequently than praise and worship. These two words occur over four hundred and fifty times in the Bible. In the Garden of Eden, Adam and Eve lived in a worship fellowship with Jehovah—until sin separated them from God. Then God instituted worship through substitutionary sacrifice.

The Scriptures begin with worship and, similarly, they end with worship. Besides showing us the way worship is now occurring in eternity, the book of Revelation contains several commands to worship God. Perhaps the most outstanding occasion is John's report:

> *And I saw another angel fly in the midst of Heaven, having the everlasting gospel to preach unto them that dwell on the earth, and to every nation, and kindred, and tongue, and people, Saying with a loud voice, Fear God, and give glory to him; for the hour of his judgment is come: and worship him that made heaven, and earth, and the sea, and the fountains of waters.*
>
> Revelation 14:6-7

The last command God gave to the inhabitants of this Earth before its complete renovation by fire was, *"Fear [worship] God, and give glory to him."* The book of Psalms, absolutely filled with injunctions to praise and worship the Lord, lies midway between these beginning and ending commands. David's cry exemplifies the heart of the Psalter. He prayed:

> *O God, thou art my God: early will I seek thee: my soul thirsteth for thee, my flesh longeth for thee in a dry and thirsty land, where no water is: To see thy power and thy glory, so as I have seen thee in the sanctuary. Because thy lovingkindness is better than life, my lips shall praise thee.* Psalm 63:1-3

David felt that the inner cry after God was an ever-pressing command to praise and worship Him.

Not only are men and women commanded to praise the Lord; even the angels of Heaven are under God's command to worship Jesus. We read:

> *And again, when he bringeth in the firstbegotten into the world, he saith, And let all the angels of God worship him.* Hebrews 1:6

With God, "let" is a command. He said, *"Let there be light: and there was light"* (Genesis 1:3). So, when God says, *"Let all the angels of God worship him,"* that is an implicit edict of the Almighty. If angels are under a divine directive to worship God, we lower creatures must definitely be commanded to worship Him too.

When we look at the Psalter, we repeatedly hear such

commands to worship the Lord. In the most courteous tones melody can supply, they command us:

> *Praise the* LORD *with harp: sing unto him with the psaltery and an instrument of ten strings.*
> Psalm 33:2

> *Trust in him at all times; ye people, pour out your heart before him: God is a refuge for us. Selah.*
> Psalm 62:8

> *Exalt the* LORD *our God, and worship at his holy hill; for the* LORD *our God is holy.* Psalm 99:9

> *Praise ye the* LORD. *O give thanks unto the* LORD, *for he is good: for his mercy endureth for ever.*
> Psalm 106:1

> *Praise ye the* LORD. *Praise, O ye servants of the* LORD, *praise the name of the* LORD. Psalm 113:1

> *All the kings of the earth shall praise thee, O* LORD, *when they hear the words of thy mouth. Yea, they shall sing in the ways of the* LORD: *for great is the glory of the* LORD. Psalm 138:4-5

Wouldn't it be glorious if we had a tape recording of these men singing these songs? These lyrics are far more than enticements to praise; they are injunctions to worship the Lord. In the gentlest terms possible, God has commanded us to praise Him, for our natures need to praise the Lord. We strengthen ourselves when we praise and worship the Lord God. Worship brings us into a fellowship with Him that allows His life to flow into our being.

Worship Directed

God not only demands that we worship, He gives us uncomplicated, yet implicit directions in our worship. He doesn't seem too concerned with our method of expression, but He is inflexible about the object of our worship.

At Mount Sinai, God entered into a covenant with the Israelites, promising to drive out the inhabitants of the Promised Land as they entered it. He prohibited their making a covenant with any of these nations:

> *Take heed to thyself, lest thou make a covenant with the inhabitants of the land whither thou goest, lest it be for a snare in the midst of thee: But ye shall destroy their altars, break their images, and cut down their groves: For thou shalt worship no other god: for the* Lord*, whose name is Jealous, is a jealous God. Lest thou make a covenant with the inhabitants of the land, and they go a-whoring after their gods, and do sacrifice unto their gods.* Exodus 34:12-15

God did not urge them to pull down, cast out, or bind the gods of the land through which they passed. He merely said to destroy the altars built to them. If this were written for today's generation, it would ask for the destruction of some books and magazines we read, a censuring of television programs we watch, and a change in the sources of amusement and pleasure we frequent. Anything that becomes the place of our veneration is an altar to a god other than Jehovah—whether it be a bank deposit, a golf course, a house, or a car.

Perhaps we need to stop trying to pull Satan and his high spirit forces out of the air and concentrate on destroying altars in our lives that could be places of worship offered to him. God's command to Israel at Sinai concentrated on worshiping Jehovah. God couples His command for exclusive worship to a fresh revelation of His nature as revealed through His names. He calls Himself Jealous. He is not a jealous Jehovah; He is Jehovah Jealous. That is His name, and His name always reveals a facet of His nature. Since He is changeless, both His nature and His commands are inviolate. All worship must go to Him—or else!

Any person married to a jealous partner has learned to guard his or her eyes and actions for the sake of peace in the marriage. Perhaps today's generation of worshipers needs to do similarly. If, in our worship sessions, we pay too much attention to Satan and his kingdom, we must deal with One whose name is Jealous, and it is a fearsome thing to deal with the jealous nature of God.

Sin does not stir God's jealousy; it invokes His mercy. Rebellion does not arouse God's jealousy; it incites His anger. It is only misdirected worship that stimulates God's jealous nature, for worship belongs exclusively to Him, and He will not allow another to have it. Jesus told Satan during the temptation in the wilderness:

> *It is written, Thou shalt worship the Lord thy God, and him only shalt thou serve.* Matthew 4:10

God has a monopoly on our worship, and He enforces that exclusivity with a passion. God's initial direction in worship was to direct all worship to Himself. When any other object, person, or being receives our worship, God credits it as "idolatry." Eulogizing the power of Satan and calling public attention to his presence (whether real or imagined) is directing worship to the wrong person.

Worship Requires Obedience

A second area of direction the Word of God gives us for worship is that it must be coupled with obedience and giving. When God was instructing the second generation of Israelites just before they entered the Promised Land, He taught them about the law of tithing. He told them that when they came into the land, they were to bring their tithe to the priests on the feast day and to say:

> *And now, behold, I have brought the first fruits of the land, which thou, O Lord, hast given me.*
>
> Deuteronomy 26:10

Then they were to worship:

> *And thou shalt set it before the Lord thy God, and worship before the Lord thy God.*
>
> Deuteronomy 26:10

God connected their obedience in giving with worship. They were to set their gift before God and then worship before Him. Is this where the Wise Men of the Gospels learned to bring gifts to be presented before the Christ-child before they worshiped Him?

Through Asaph, the psalmist, God said:

> *Hear, O my people, and I will testify unto thee. O Israel, if thou wilt hearken unto me, There shall no strange god be in thee; neither shalt thou worship any strange god.* Psalm 81:8-9

God promised His people protection from inner influences of any false spirit seeking worship, but He also commanded them to maintain the discipline of exclusively worshiping Him. These rules were amplified, not rescinded, by Jesus in the wilderness temptation.

The two most important directions God gives in worshiping Him is to first direct everything to Him and, second, to worship in honest obedience.

Worship Demonstrated

The three Hebrew children displayed determination to worship Jehovah alone—no matter what the consequences might be. Threatened with death unless they worshiped the golden image Nebuchadnezzar had erected, they refused to bow or bend to this massive idol. Consequently the king had them thrown into the fiery furnace. God, however, stepped into the fire with them and preserved their lives. When they stepped out of the oven, it was without so much as the smell of smoke on them:

> *Then Nebuchadnezzar spake, and said, Blessed be the God of Shadrach, Meshach, and Abednego, who hath sent his angel, and delivered his servants that trusted*

in him, and have changed the king's word, and yielded their bodies, that they might not serve nor worship any god, except their own God. Daniel 3:28

If exclusive worship of God has a price set on it, we must pay that price. Millions of martyrs before us have refused to love their lives to the death, and so must we.

We learn so much about worship from the singers of Israel. In their psalms, they speak often of the Spirit's command to worship the Lord, and their emphasis is always on directing those responses exclusively to God. Listen to these men sing:

All the ends of the world shall remember and turn unto the LORD: and all the kindreds of the nations shall worship before thee. Psalm 22:27

Give unto the LORD the glory due unto his name; worship the LORD in the beauty of holiness. Psalm 29:2

All the earth shall worship thee, and shall sing unto thee, they shall sing to thy name. Selah. Psalm 66:4

All nations whom thou hast made shall come and worship before thee, O LORD: and shall glorify thy name. Psalm 86:9

O come, let us worship and bow down. Let us kneel before the LORD our maker. Psalm 95:6

O worship the LORD in the beauty of holiness: fear before him, all the earth. Psalm 96:9

Exalt the L*ORD our God, and worship at his footstool; for He is holy.* Psalm 99:5

The admonition and example put forth in the Psalms consistently emphasize that worship belongs exclusively to Jehovah God. These men of music and song were not the only writers in the Holy Bible to see this exclusivity in worship. The prophets also declared it. They wrote:

It shall come to pass, that from one new moon to another, and from one sabbath to another, shall all flesh come to worship before me, saith the LORD.
Isaiah 66:23

And it shall come to pass, that every one that is left of all the nations which came against Jerusalem shall even go up from year to year to worship the King, the LORD *of hosts, and to keep the feast of tabernacles.*
Zechariah 14:16

Who shall not fear thee, O LORD, *and glorify thy name? for thou only art holy: for all nations shall come and worship before thee; for thy judgments are made manifest.* Revelation 15:4

In the New Testament, the Apostle Paul was a dynamic demonstration of worship. From the day of his conversion until the hour of his death, he was a worshiper of God, bent on obeying every word the Lord spoke to him. At his trial before Felix, he confessed to both him and the high priest and elders from Jerusalem:

This I confess unto thee, that after the way which they call heresy, so worship I the God of my fathers, believing all things which are written in the law and in the prophets. Acts 24:14

Paul had a single eye to worship. He couldn't stand religious pretensions or cold, dead dogma. He worshiped the living Christ with such exclusivity that he found himself in trouble with religious leaders everywhere he went. God help us to shed the old garments of religion past and clothe ourselves with the new garments of praise. They will enable us to obey the scriptural admonition:

Be filled with the Spirit; Speaking to yourselves in psalms and hymns and spiritual songs, singing and making melody in your heart to the Lord; Giving thanks always for all things unto God and the Father in the name of our Lord Jesus Christ.

Ephesians 5:18-20

In teaching us the proper use of the gift of prophecy, Paul says:

And thus are the secrets of his heart made manifest; and so falling down on his face he will worship God, and report that God is in you of a truth.

1 Corinthians 14:25

The gifts of the Spirit are marvelous tools of worship. They stir the hearts of observers to render praise to God, and they release the heart of the worshiper to Him. God did not give us these gifts to enable us to draw attention to the demonic. They came to magnify the divine and help us in our responses to the Almighty.

It hardly takes a Bible scholar to realize that not all worship is worship of God. Even Christians can worship something short of God. The Bible speaks of four major reasons our worship goes astray:

1. Deliberate departure from God
2. Deception from the wicked one
3. Doctrines embraced above God's Word
4. Dedication to men that is higher than dedication to God

Deliberate departure from God generally brings us to worship something we have created. The prophet declared of Israel:

> *Their land also is full of idols; they worship the work of their own hands, that which their own fingers have made.* Isaiah 2:8

Worshiping our own creation, whether the idols are metal or mental, is idolatrous. It will always bring the judgment of God upon us.

Deception, whether inspired by demons or men, will lead our worship away from God. God told His chosen people:

> *Take heed to yourselves, that your heart be not deceived, and ye turn aside, and serve other gods, and worship them.* Deuteronomy 11:16

I honestly fear that in the extreme emphasis common today in spiritual warfare, the devil has deceived the minds of many to believe they are worshiping God, when, in fact, they are directing all their attention, energies, and worship to the devil.

Doctrines can so strongly control our minds that we observe them more than we obey God. Jesus warned:

> *But in vain they do worship me, teaching for doctrines the commandments of men.* Matthew 15:9

Are we blindly following doctrines that lack scriptural validity? If so, our worship is in vain. It does not reach God's throne.

Dedication to men that is higher than our dedication to God is one of the greatest perversions of worship. As holy a man as the Apostle John was, at least three times he fell at the feet of the angel who was conducting him through the visions of Heaven and tried to worship him. John admits:

> *And I fell at his feet to worship him. And he said unto me, See thou do it not: I am thy fellowservant, and of thy brethren that have the testimony of Jesus: worship God: for the testimony of Jesus is the spirit of prophecy.* Revelation 19:10

Because of the popularity or spiritual power of a certain man or woman, we often blindly follow him or her into error in our worship. How frequently have I heard it said: "It doesn't seem right to me, but he is a good man," or "She is a recognized teacher and who am I to judge?" According to the Bible, you must judge all teaching by the inspired Word of God. Telling God you were following recognized religious leaders will not be an acceptable excuse in the Day of Judgment.

In these final days before the return of Christ, we dare not deliberately turn to idolatry. We dare not allow our hearts to be deceived. We must strengthen our knowledge of the Word of God so we cannot be led astray by doctrines that look like they are from God, but lack a biblical foundation. Finally, may God deliver us from blind dedication to what seemingly good men and women teach. The Word of God is our measuring rod, not the popularity of men. The Apostle Paul warned:

> *But though we, or an angel from heaven, preach any other gospel unto you than that which we have preached unto you, let him be accursed.*
>
> Galatians 1:8

Praise and worship are not optional. They are obligatory. Worship is not something God merely commends; it is something He has commanded. While God grants great latitude in where, when, and how to worship, He offers no personal choice in who to worship. God is the only acceptable object of our worship. Let us never be guilty of coming together to extol the negative virtues of the devil and sing and shout about his power. That would be worship of the wrong person, and we desire our worship to exalt our Lord Jesus Christ.

To Him be praise forevermore.
Amen!